As Long As I Have You

Jeanette Gilge

© 1998 by Jeanette Gilge-Barnes. All rights reserved

Printed in the United States of America

Packaged by WinePress Publishing, PO Box 1406, Mukilteo, WA 98275. The views expressed or implied in this work do not necessarily reflect those of WinePress Publishing. Ultimate design, content, and editorial accuracy of this work is the responsibility of the author(s).

No part of this publication may be reproduced, stored in a retrieval system or transmitted in any way by any means, electronic, mechanical, photocopy, recording or otherwise, without the prior permission of the copyright holder except as provided by USA copyright law.

ISBN 1-57921-140-2
Library of Congress Catalog Card Number: 98-61050

In loving memory of Kenny.

One

The raw wind whistled down Armitage Street and cut through Jeanie's threadbare gray coat like it was cheesecloth. She wrapped it around her slim body, ducked her head, and hurried on. January in Chicago, she had discovered, was no more pleasant than in northern Wisconsin.

She skirted a group of plodding fellow workers and ran to catch the streetcar grinding down California Avenue. With her seven cents clutched in her hand, she swung aboard the car, ahead of the crowd when it stopped.

An empty seat—right near the front. If she caught a car without having to wait at North Avenue, she might beat Kenny home. It would be nice to be able to wash her face and slip into a dress that did not smell like oil before he kissed her.

She stretched her legs and wiggled her toes in her brown loafers. Sitting down was sheer bliss after standing eight hours at the big, old, black machines that twisted nylon yarn used to make parachute cords.

A girl with light brown hair was sitting in front of her, and Jeanie stared at the soft, loose curls, wondering if her hair was about the same color. She suspected that sunshine would bring out red highlights.

Jeanie was, in fact, quite pleased with her own hair color—a sharp contrast with the way she felt about her gray blue eyes, her short upper lip, and her nose that needed to tilt up a bit.

No matter how many times Kenny told her she was beautiful, or how many truck drivers whistled at her, she still felt plain. And even though her clear, lightly freckled skin gleaned many compliments, she would cancel them out, much as Gram used to do, by concentrating on her imperfections.

But now, even though she was aware she was not as attractive as pretty, dark-haired Marge at work or Kenny's cute little sister, Vi, it didn't matter. Kenny thought she was beautiful and loved her.

She couldn't wait to get home.

At North Avenue she caught a car immediately, but there was no seat this time. As the car lurched forward, she clung to the handle on the corner of a seat and stared out at Humboldt Park, now brown and drab. A few dry leaves played tag around the black tree trunks on the ugly, dead turf. At least in Wisconsin they had snow to mercifully hide the naked earth.

But tonight it didn't matter that the outside was dull and drab. Their little attic apartment would be warm and bright and filled with love and laughter. There had better not be too much laughter, though.

She held back a giggle as she thought about last night.

CHAPTER ONE

It had been Kenny's turn to make up the hide-a-bed, and when he leaned over, it took only a little shove to send him sprawling on his face.

He sprang up shouting, "I'll get you!" and she led the chase into the kitchen, around the table, and back into the living room. He almost cornered her behind a rocker, but she slipped past him and charged back into the kitchen. That was when he knocked over the end table, and sent a stack of coasters and the alarm clock clattering to the floor.

Amid their peals of laughter, they suddenly heard a loud knock on the door leading to the downstairs apartment.

Since Kenny was only in his underwear, Jeanie hastily tucked in her blouse and opened the door.

Mr. Rassmussen, the elderly landlord, stood panting on the second stair, his gnarled hand trembling on the doorframe. "Are you all right? Is that young man beating you?"

"Oh! No, I'm sorry," Jeanie answered breathlessly. "We were just a . . . goofing around."

She caught a glimpse of the landlady's anxious face peering up from the downstairs doorway.

Jeanie opened a bobby pin with her teeth and pinned back her hair, all the while explaining that Kenny had been leaning over the bed and . . .

The old man gave her a you-don't-have-to-explain wave and said, "We were afraid you were fighting." He turned to go downstairs, a smile tugging at the corners of his mouth.

"We never fight," she called after him. She wanted to tell him that time was too precious, that Kenny could get his draft notice any day. But she was afraid she'd cry. Anyway, it was not necessary. Every time she met her landlord, he gave her a searching look, as if to ask if that notice had come.

7

As Long as I Have You

At Kedzie Avenue, someone got off the streetcar, and Jeanie sat down. It still bothered her that the Rassmussens would think she and Kenny were fighting. But the old people had known them only since September. She counted on her fingers. September, October, November, December, January. Today was the seventh. Nineteen more days and they would be married four whole months.

She stood up at Central Park and worked her way to the door. In the front seat, a man was reading a newspaper, and she saw the huge headline: PRESIDENT ANNOUNCES AMERICAN CASUALTIES EXCEED 60,000.

Whenever she read headlines like that, she caught her breath until the cold chill passed. The image of those deadly words sharp in her mind, she hopped off the streetcar at Lawndale and ran to the corner. She cut diagonally across Concord Place—a little dead-end street—through the gangway, and up the winding outdoor stairs to their little crow's-nest apartment.

The door was open and that meant Kenny was home. Her disappointment of not being able to freshen up melted the moment she saw him silhouetted against the sheer, white front-room curtains.

"Hi," she called as she took off her coat. "I caught the North Avenue car right away. I thought for once I might beat you home.

He did not return her greeting. Instead, he silently handed her an opened letter.

She caught her breath when she saw an official-looking seal at the top next to the date: DECEMBER 31, 1942. The next line was dark and bold: ORDER TO REPORT FOR INDUCTION. She sank down on the hide-a-bed before she read, "The president of the United States, to . . ." Kenny's name was

CHAPTER ONE

typed in along with an order number. "Greeting," she read. Some greeting. She skipped the fine print, as well as the address of the draft board, searching for the time and date he was to report: 6:30 A.M., JANUARY 15, 1943.

There was more fine print but her vision was too blurred to read it.

"A week from tomorrow," Kenny said.

She was about to get up on rubbery legs and throw her arms around him, when he walked into the kitchen without so much as a glance, grabbed the garbage can, and headed out the door.

The letter fell to the floor, and Jeanie broke into sobs. *One more week, and he walks away. How could he? Didn't he know she wanted to stay in his arms every second until the time they were torn apart? Didn't he care?*

When he came back upstairs, she was staring at the floor. "Hey! When do we eat?" he called to her from the kitchen.

She remained motionless. *How could he even think about eating?*

She heard him rummaging in the pantry, and reluctantly, silently she went to get the leftover chili from the little pantry window that served as a refrigerator.

"You pray," he said when they sat down to eat.

She shook her head.

So he prayed the "Come-Lord-Jesus-be-our-guest" prayer and began to eat.

"Come on, Jeanie," he urged, when her hands remained in her lap. "We knew this was coming ever since they dropped the draft age down to eighteen last November. And it isn't the end of the world, you know."

She pushed back her chair and ran to the front room. Sobbing, she threw herself across the hide-a-bed. Surely he would come and take her in his arms.

He stayed in the kitchen.

When she heard him washing dishes, she crept into the kitchen, elbowed him aside, and took over without a word.

But, instead of staying beside her, as she had hoped, he went into the front room, turned on the radio, and was even heartless enough to laugh at Charlie McCarthy's silly jokes.

She nibbled a cracker as she finished drying the dishes, then she dumped her pay envelope onto the table and counted out seven dollars. "We have to pay rent tonight," she called to him.

"Go do it!" he answered.

"I can't," she said. "I'll cry."

His jaw tight, he snatched up the money and ran downstairs.

Later in bed, he turned to gather her in his arms, but she jerked away.

He sat up, lit a cigarette, and took a long draw on it before he said, "What's the matter with you? We have a week left—maybe a little more if I get a furlough after I get inducted—and you pull this stuff. I don't get it."

She curled into an angry ball. He knew how much she hated his smoking, especially right before they went to bed. She coughed and pulled the blanket over her head.

"How do you think *I* feel?" he muttered.

Her head popped out. "That's what I'd like to know. You act like you don't even care."

Abruptly he stubbed out his cigarette, rolled over and drew her close. "You want me to lay around and cry with you, is that it?"

"Well . . ."

"Hey! I'm supposed to be a soldier, remember? I'm supposed to be brave. How am I going to go out there and fight if I can't even handle getting my draft notice?"

CHAPTER ONE

Her body relaxed against his.

"Oh, Baby!" he said tenderly, "I don't want to leave you. These months have been the happiest months of my life. But we gotta get this war over. You wouldn't want me to be a draft dodger."

"I wouldn't care if you were."

He shook her gently. "Oh yes, you would. Honey, I know they can win that war without me, but by golly, I want to do all I can to help get it over fast, so we can start really living. And now you gotta help me. I'm not so brave, you know," he said with a catch in his voice.

She pressed her wet cheek against his. It was wet too.

Two

The next morning on the streetcar, people read their newspapers, some dozed, and a few, who probably knew each other, held conversations just like every other day.

Jeanie huddled against the window thinking, *Don't they know my world has fallen apart?* She was suddenly aware that she was now, and would continue to be, alone in her grief. It was like she was in a little storm-tossed boat, struggling to stay afloat, while unheeding oceanliners glided by. Ah, but there was a safe harbor ahead at work. Margie would care and maybe even some of the older ladies.

Walking down Armitage Street, Jeanie determined to be brave for Margie's sake. Her husband, John, was deferred because he was employed in vital war work, but it was unlikely he would be deferred the second time. Margie needed to see that one could go on. All the while Jeanie changed into her navy blue apron, Jeanie told herself to simply state the fact when she saw Margie and walk calmly to her machines.

Margie was hanging her clothes in her locker when Jeanie came out of the washroom. Taking one look at Jeanie, Margie let out a little cry. "Oh no, Kenny got his notice."

Two steps and Margie's arms were around her, and Jeanie was sobbing on Margie's shoulder.

"I wanted to be so brave," Jeanie said shakily, drying her eyes.

"Just keep a shoulder ready," Margie said, handing her a dry Kleenex, "I'll need one too."

By the way the older ladies looked at her, Jeanie knew word had spread. Once, when two of them thought they were alone in the washroom, she heard them talking about which was the most painful: having a husband or a son go off to war. A number of them already had service flags, with a blue star hanging in their front windows for each son serving. Thank goodness none of them had a gold star—yet.

Shortly before noon, Margie stopped at Jeanie's machine and said, "Have you seen the new girl? Her name's Pat. Is it all right if I ask her to eat lunch with us?"

Jeanie shrugged. "I guess so."

Margie gave her a one-arm hug. "I know this is a rough day for you, but we know how left out we felt when we came here, because all the older ladies had their own little groups."

Jeanie nodded. "Sure, go ahead. Ask her."

It was always a welcome relief when the noisy machines were shut off at noon. In warm weather, she and Margie would sit on the fire escape to eat lunch, but now they pulled stools together by a silent machine.

"She looks friendly," Jeanie said as she and Margie watched the new girl walk toward them. Her straight, blond hair made her long, narrow face look even longer.

CHAPTER TWO

She smiled and began talking even before she reached them. "Boy, am I glad you asked me to eat with you." She sat down and pulled a sandwich out of a brown bag. "Looks like the older ladies stick together."

Margie chuckled. "That they do. But some of them are really nice."

Just then Rose, one of the older ladies, patted Jeanie's shoulder as she walked by. Tears filled Jeanie's eyes. Quietly, Margie explained to Pat that Jeanie's husband had just received his draft notice.

"Oh gosh, I'm sorry," Pat said. "I'm not married, but I can imagine how you feel. How long have you been married?"

Jeanie blinked hard. "Since September 26."

"How come he wasn't drafted before?" Pat asked. "Just about all the guys I know are gone."

"He's only nineteen," Jeanie explained. "How come you're working here?" Jeanie asked, deliberately changing the subject. "You look like you belong in an office."

Pat giggled. "That's what I was thinking about you. Why aren't you two in an office?

Jeanie took a bite of her bologna sandwich and gave Margie a sidelong glance.

"Oh, we love the smell of oil and grease and hot motors," teased Margie, "and we'd be lost without the noise." She unwrapped a sandwich. "Seriously, my husband will probably be drafted soon too, and I'm trying to earn a few dollars before I go back to Nebraska."

Pat nodded and turned questioningly to Jeanie. "Well, in high school I got terrible grades in typing, and I'm scared I might have to type." She hung her head. "I hope I never have to type again as long as I live."

Pat nodded sympathetically. "I'm afraid of office work too. I didn't get to finish high school, 'cause my family needed help." Suddenly Jeanie knew she'd like Pat. Here was a city girl who didn't pretend to know everything.

"What in the world do you use on your skin?" Margie asked Pat, obviously attempting to ease the tension. "It's absolutely flawless."

Pat flushed. "Thanks. Just soap and water."

"That's what Jeanie uses," Margie said, "and she certainly has nice skin. Guess I'll have to try it."

"Oh, you," Jeanie chided. "There is nothing wrong with your skin—your whole face for that matter." She turned to Pat. "Don't you think she could be a model?"

Margie giggled and patted her ample hips. "And what do you suggest I use for a body?"

"You could borrow Jeanie's," Pat suggested.

It was Jeanie's turn to blush. She pointed to Pat's slim ankles. "And your legs."

It felt good to laugh.

Margie folded her lunch bag to use again and said, "I have to make a phone call. Don't say anything interesting while I'm gone."

Pat watched Margie walk away and sighed. "What I wouldn't give for a face like that."

Pat certainly could not be called pretty, but already Jeanie was less aware of her close-set eyes and her long face. There was a serenity about her that Jeanie envied.

"The floor-lady told me this stuff is used to make parachute cords," Pat said, looking up at the rows of big, white nylon cones and the yarn running down the machines and onto large spools.

CHAPTER TWO

Jeanie nodded. "That's what they tell us, but we don't see the finished cords here. What we do is just part of the process."

"That's good enough. At least we know we're doing something to help the war effort. Two of my brothers are in the Air Corps."

By the time the whistle blew, Jeanie knew that Pat grew up in Chicago and had four brothers and two sisters, and Pat knew that Jeanie grew up in Wisconsin and that her grandmother that reared her, because Jeanie's mother had died when she was a few weeks old. Jeanie also knew she was glad Pat had come to work in this smelly old factory.

Three

Saturday morning they made a deal: Kenny would wash the kitchen and bathroom floors, while Jeanie wrote letters to his parents and to her grandmother.

With several copies of *Woman's Day* magazine to support her stationery, she curled up on the sofa so she would be out of his way.

Taking her time, she addressed the envelopes and stuck on three-cent stamps.

"Dearest Daddy and Mother," she wrote.

"Maybe I should wait until next week," she called to Kenny. "In case you don't pass the physical."

"Are you kidding? Why wouldn't I pass the physical?"

She sighed. "Well, you never know. I'm glad you didn't have your notice when we were home at Christmas; it would have been so much harder to say good-bye."

He called from the bathroom, "Quit stalling and write those letters."

She did.

That afternoon they needed some diversion, so they walked up North Avenue to the Tiffin Theater. It would be good to watch a movie and forget about the war for a while.

But neither of them thought about the newsreel that always came before the main feature. Jeanie hid her face against Kenny's shoulder as the camera flashed scenes from the North African and South Pacific battles and the devastation in England from all those bombs.

When the cartoon came on, Jeanie fled to the restroom. Crying silently didn't give her all the relief she needed, but it did ease the ache in her throat.

On Sunday, they went to services at the church Kenny's sister, Vi, and her family attended whenever the three little ones were well or Art was not working. They were not there today, so afterward Kenny and Jeanie walked the few blocks to their house on Mozart Street.

They were barely in the door, when three-year-old Merle Ann made a dash for Kenny, and he swooped her up. Since she had been flower girl at their wedding and had made the all-night train ride with Kenny the night before the wedding, there was a special bond between them. "Someday we'll tell her she was with us on our honeymoon," Jeanie said, referring to Merle Ann's ride back on the train with them the day after the wedding.

"You're just in time," Vi said, pulling a macaroni-and-ground-beef casserole out of the oven.

"Mmm, smells good." Jeanie exclaimed, and set two more places at the white, porcelain-topped table.

When Art came to the table in a starched, blue shirt, Jeanie knew he was getting ready to go to work.

Jeanie cast an anxious glance at Kenny, wondering if he would wait until after dinner to tell them about his draft notice.

CHAPTER THREE

"Got my draft notice. Gotta go next Friday," he announced abruptly as he picked up two-year-old Buddy.

Vi gasped. "Next Friday! That isn't even a week."

"Oh, I'll probably get a week's furlough," he said. "The guys at work did when they were drafted."

Jeanie didn't dare look at Vi, fearing they'd both cry.

Art put one-year-old Billy in the high chair and didn't say a word.

Jeanie sat down and kept her eyes on her plate.

Vi broke the strained silence. "It's a good thing you didn't have your notice when you were home for Christmas," she said softly. "If they knew you'd be going . . ." She couldn't finish the sentence.

Jeanie nodded. "That's what I told him."

The men switched the conversation to the New Year's football games, and Vi and Jeanie sat silent.

"Gotta get to work," Art said, scraping back his chair. He pulled on his streetcar conductor's jacket, grabbed his cap, kissed the little ones, and then dramatically swept pretty little Vi into his arms. "Try to survive without me, Dear. You, too," he told Jeanie, kissing her lightly. He pretended he was going to kiss Kenny, and Kenny cuffed him on the shoulder. Jeanie joined the laughter, but her throat still ached.

They soon left so Vi and the little ones could nap. Walking home, the afternoon and evening stretched uneventfully ahead of them. Neither wanted to talk about Kenny's departure and the last-minute practical things they must do. In fact, there was very little to do. He would need only the clothes he wore, and there was nothing that Jeanie could not handle by herself when he was gone. She simply had the rent to pay each week, which included the gas and elec-

21

tricity, each week. They avoided conversation about the distant future and clung to the here-and-now.

Back at their apartment that afternoon, they listened to the radio while cuddled on the hide-a-bed. Kenny closed his eyes, and Jeanie studied his profile, trying to lock every precious detail into her memory. She wanted to brush back the wave of ash blonde hair that fell over his forehead, but resisted the impulse. Would he change while he was gone? Would those heavy eyebrows become even heavier? How many times had those gently curved lips touched hers? A sob caught in her throat. She swallowed hard and concentrated on his strong, masculine chin.

She saw him smile when "Lilacs in the Rain" began playing on the radio. "Every time I hear that," he said, "I think of Johnny O'Brien and the little band we had when I was a senior."

"Uh-huh," she murmured. "He was one of the first teachers to go off to war after Pearl Harbor."

"Wonder where he is now."

"Mr. Spielel went too, you know."

"Yeah!" Kenny chuckled. "And if he gets as mad at those Nazis as he used to get at us in band, this war will be over in no time."

Jeanie chuckled her agreement. "Remember? He'd actually turn purple."

So many memories, she thought. They had been a couple for over four years, although the past winter she was in Wisconsin attending high school, and he was working in Chicago. She burrowed her face into his neck, remembering the pain of that lonely school term. And now how long would it be? The ache in her throat was unbearable. She concentrated on remembering how it felt to be close to him.

CHAPTER THREE

She absorbed the deep beat of his heart and the slow rise and fall of his chest and the scent of his after-shave lotion.

What is he thinking, she wondered. *Does he see himself crouched in a foxhole like those soldiers in the newsreel? Or crawling across a mine field?*

"What are you thinking about?" she whispered.

He grinned. "I was thinking we should make potato pancakes. I'll peel 'em and grate 'em, if you fry 'em." He dumped her off the bed and followed her into the kitchen.

"I found out why your mother's potato pancakes are better than my grandma's," Jeanie said from the small under-the-eaves pantry. "She drains off all the potato water, so it doesn't take so much flour."

"Umm! Good." Kenny exclaimed when he had taken the first bite of a crisp-edged pancake.

"Remember how you told people at our wedding, 'We're going to live on love and potato pancakes?'"

He nodded, but he didn't look at her. Under that blustery exterior beat a tender heart. She knew that now.

At noon the next day, Margie, Pat, and Jeanie pulled stools together, and Jeanie reached into her brown bag. "What on earth!" She pulled out two waxed-paper-wrapped rolls. When she opened one, there lay a cold, gray potato pancake with a sprinkling of sugar and several lumps of butter.

"Oh no, Kenny made lunches last night, and I didn't even look to see what he was doing. He *loves* cold potato pancakes." She wrinkled her nose. "All I have beside are two windmill cookies and an apple. I guess I'll have to eat 'em."

"They do look pretty awful," Margie said. "But they probably taste good."

Pat laughed and watched as Jeanie nibbled a stiff pancake.

23

"Hmm, not too bad." Jeanie giggled. "I guess he was right when he told people at our wedding that we were going to live on love and potato pancakes."

"He sounds like a lot of fun," Pat said. "Do you have a picture of him?"

Jeanie bounded up and dug her wallet out of her handbag. She handed Pat a small, black-and-white snapshot of her and Kenny, taken the previous summer.

"Oh my goodness, you're taller than he is. I wouldn't even consider dating a boy who was shorter than me."

The silence hung heavy as Jeanie took the snapshot and put it back in her wallet.

"Oh, Jeanie, I'm sorry," Pat said, "I'm always saying tactless things. My mother says I was born with my foot in my mouth. He really is cute."

"It's all right. I can't say I wouldn't like it if he were taller, but he probably wishes I had a straight nose, too."

Pat leaned closer. "What's wrong with your nose?"

"I fell on a coaster sled when I was little and must have broken it."

"I hadn't even noticed," Pat said.

"That's just what I told her," Margie interjected. "I didn't notice it until she mentioned it."

There was silence for a moment as Jeanie wondered how she could let Pat know she wasn't offended. Then she said, "You aren't the first one to remark about Kenny's height, Pat. Sometimes I tell 'em that I know a lot of six-footers I wouldn't want to live with for one day."

Margie chuckled. "I like that. Really, when you think of it, if we love a guy only because of the way he looks, what happens if he changes, if he gets hurt or something?"

Chapter Three

Scenes of wounded soldiers from yesterday's newsreel flashed before Jeanie's eyes. She put her remaining cookie back in the bag.

All afternoon she struggled with thoughts about wounded and disfigured men. She remembered when she was about ten and saw a man with only one leg at the county fair. Her stomach was in a knot the rest of the day.

God, please don't let Kenny get hurt. I think I could love him no matter what, but it would be so awful for him.

She thought about Ray, Kenny's brother who was in the infantry. He hoped to get into officer's training, but Kenny's mother said she hoped he didn't, because infantry officers were in the most danger.

The afternoon dragged as Jeanie took off fat, white spools and put on empty ones and prayed that Kenny wouldn't be assigned to the infantry.

Emma looked out the window again. Today was only Tuesday—too early for a letter from Jeanie, but watching for the mail carrier's car had become as much a habit for Emma as it was for her to wash her dishes as soon as she finished eating, or to braid her long, gray hair before she went to bed, or to sweep the floor of her kitchen/living room after breakfast.

When she saw him come down the hill, stop at the mailbox, and drive away, she pulled on her galoshes, tied on her *Kopftuch*, and buttoned her old, gray tweed coat close at the neck.

On her way out, she brushed the snow off a stretch of porch railing and scattered some bread crumbs for the chickadees. *Poor little things. How could they live in below-zero weather?*

Her white breath floated behind her like a filmy scarf, and she could feel the crunch of the snow under her feet, although she could no longer hear it.

She smiled up at the blue sky and the tops of the pine and spruce trees that formed a windbreak along the road. It was good to be out in the fresh, cold air for a little while. But, as her nose began to sting with cold, she prayed for her sons, Roy and Carl, out logging all day. *Lord, don't let their noses and ears freeze.*

In the mailbox, she found several letters for Roy and Helen and a letter for herself from Jeanie.

She hurried back to the house. She didn't expect a letter today. Usually it came every Wednesday because Jeanie wrote every Sunday, but here was a letter on Tuesday.

In the house, she took off her outdoor clothes and put on her felt bedroom slippers before she allowed herself to carefully cut off the end of Jeanie's envelope.

She settled herself in the rocker and shook out the letter.

Dear Gram,

Oh, Mama. [She always called Gram Mama when she was feeling emotional] Kenny got his draft notice. He has to go for his physical next Friday. I wish he wouldn't pass it, but I don't want anything to be wrong with him. We knew it was coming, but now that we know when he'll go, I just want to die! I don't want him to see me crying all the time, but I can't help it. Why does it have to hurt so much to love?

Chapter Three

Emma had to pull a handkerchief out of her apron pocket and dry her eyes before she could read on. *Poor little girl. Poor little girl.*

Emma's hands dropped to her lap, and she rested her head against the back of the rocker. Just children, those two, but so much in love. She smiled as she remembered the morning after their wedding. They wanted to spend their wedding night at the hotel in Tomahawk, but without a car, they ended up staying in Jeanie's room.

Emma wanted them to have a good breakfast before they left for the train, so she went to wake them a little before nine. Her eyes filled again, thinking of how they slept— clinging to each other as if to defy anything on earth to tear them apart.

And now, they would be apart for who-knows-how-long. She sighed as she thought of all her grandsons already in service: Paul, Art, Kermit, Everett, Clyde, Earl, Al, Gordon, Glen, John, and maybe a few more she had not yet heard about. Most of them were single, so young women were spared the hurt, but she ached for their parents—her own children.

It was at times like this when Emma would feel a sudden surge of anger because of her hearing loss. How she wished she could phone her daughters: Ella, Gertie, Minnie, or her daughter-in-law, Olga. Oh, she could go in the other part of the house and talk with Helen, but Helen was young and centered on her own five little ones. She had yet to understand the pain of bidding a child good-bye. And of course, talking meant that Helen had to shout in Emma's ear and probably wake up baby Gene in the process.

But there is always someone to talk with. There is always Jesus. What would she do if she could not have that ongoing conversation with Him? At times she was sure He spoke to her in her thoughts, but she would never tell anybody that. That only happened back in Bible days, she had been told.

Helen's kitchen was empty. She must be upstairs. Emma laid the letter on her kitchen table.

Back in her part of the house, Emma picked up her knitting, positioned herself over her rocker, bent her seventy-four-year-old knees as far as they would go, and dropped the remaining few inches to the seat.

It would be a relief to be able to cry out to God about the pain she felt for Jeanie and Kenny, but it settled deep in her being, beyond the reach of tears. Just the thought of an army uniform brought back the anguish of the First World War, when her young son Ed had been wounded twice in France. It brought back the memory of the waiting. Waiting for news, and then that almost intolerable wait those many months after the war ended for him to come home in time to see his dying father.

It was a miracle, the doctor said, that Al hung on to life that summer. But even Red Cross help had been in vain, and Al had been gone six weeks when Ed came home.

She sighed, now remembering that her predominate emotion had been an incredible sense of relief to know Al was out of agony. Those two years of agony had seemed like a century, as they tried in every way to ease his pain, as he lay in the narrow bedroom.

She hardly gained her emotional balance, when Emmie, her joy—her precious, young schoolteacher-daughter, married hastily, quit teaching at Christmas, and gave birth to fragile little Jeanie the last day of March. A few days later,

CHAPTER THREE

fever raging, Emmie was loaded into the baggage car of the train and taken to Ashland hospital sixty miles away.

Oh, the prayers, the anguished waiting again. When Jeanie was five weeks old, Emma went to visit Emmie, and they both agreed that Emma must take baby Jeanie home. "You took good care of us," Emmie said. "You'll take good care of her, too." Emma later learned that Ed, Jeanie's father, had promised he would never take her away from Emma.

It was then—while trying to manage the farm with the help of the three youngest boys, and trying to work while the baby cried incessantly—that Emma felt the full impact of Al's absence.

In a way, she was grateful that he didn't have to bear the grief of losing their ever-smiling, tenderhearted Emmie.

But even worse than the grief, was the bitterness that welled up in her, the awful thoughts that assaulted her. She would look at that pathetic, eczema-covered baby and think, *If it weren't for you, Emmie would be alive.* She never allowed those thoughts to linger, but she cringed with guilt whenever they came into her mind.

Thanks to young Roy, who took over management of the farm, the dairy herd increased, and there were several good years before the Great Depression. On its heels came the terrible drought.

How many times, Emma wondered, had she remarked that it was more difficult to rear Jeanie than all the other thirteen children put together. Only last spring she realized how painful it was for Jeanie to so often hear that. She tried so hard—too hard—to rear Jeanie to become everything Emmie would have wanted her to be.

If Emmie were alive, what would she do now? she wondered. Surely she would accept and love Kenny as Emma

29

did. Emmie would delight in those blue eyes that never shifted away from one's gaze. She would find joy at his teasing, his laughter, and most of all, his adoration of Jeanie. Surely she would approve of their marriage, as Emma did, even though Jeanie was only eighteen and Kenny a few days shy of nineteen.

Emma was aware that, from the world's point of view, Kenny had little to offer—only a high school education, no savings, no skills. Yet Emma knew these two would struggle and grow together, as they already had these last four years. It had been time they marry, and she could understand Jeanie's desire for their home to be established before he went off to war.

She sighed. A lot of good it would have done to have tried to stop them. Would it hurt any less for them to be parted if they weren't married?

The yarn still around her finger, Emma realized that her knitting lay idle in her lap. The needles clicked again, unheard by her, as she picked up, not only her knitting, but also the threads of her life.

Enough of the past. There was living to do. She must get her mind back on other family members and not just focus on Jeanie's troubles. It wasn't difficult with so much family around her. Roy and Helen and the five children were under the same roof with her. And Hank and Buelah, Al and Mamie, Carl and Olga, Henry and Ella, and George and Sadie all lived around the same mile-square block. Joe and Gertie, Nels and Minnie, Len and Nora, and John and Esther all lived within an hour's drive. Only Fred and Helen and Ed and Peggy lived farther away. How fortunate she was.

But she certainly wouldn't ignore Jeanie's pain. *Father,* she whispered, *show me how to give her courage.*

Four

Friday morning, before the alarm rang, Jeanie heard Mr. Rassmussen scooping coal into the furnace. A shock raced through her when she realized it was the day Kenny had to report for induction. She tried to console herself by remembering that this was really only a dress rehearsal for the real good-bye next Friday. But fearful thoughts kept coming. *What if he didn't get a week's furlough before he left? What if he had to leave today?* Her teeth chattered as she threw on a robe, made coffee, and poured canned grapefruit juice for Kenny.

He gave her a fresh-shave kiss, and she clung to him. "What if you don't get to come home today?" The words barely squeezed past the lump in her throat.

"I'll be home," he assured her.

The day at work dragged as Jeanie's thoughts raced from one chilling *what if* to another. She told herself that if Kenny did leave today, they wouldn't have to say good-bye again next week, but that was no consolation. She wanted to be

31

with him every possible minute. She couldn't wait to get home.

Of course, she had to wait for a streetcar at North Avenue and wait again as it got caught by every red light. Her jaws ached with tension.

Finally, when she ran up the stairs to their apartment, there was Kenny—peeling potatoes.

As they held each other, her heart thudded against his chest. After several long kisses he released her, and she studied his sober face.

"I'm in," he said, and went back to the potatoes.

She choked out the words, "When do you have to go?"

"Next Friday morning—6:30 again."

"Same place?"

He shook his head. "It's about half a block from where you work."

Jeanie groaned. "Oh, no! I've seen men out there waiting for a bus. I never thought you'd have to report there, because it's so far from here."

"I'll be gone long before you go to work," he assured her. "We can say good-bye at home."

They decided to keep working that week even though they wanted to spend every moment together. "It will be better if we're busy," Kenny insisted. Reluctantly, Jeanie agreed.

The week sped by and it was Friday morning again. Even though the landlord stoked the furnace, and the rooms were warm, Jeanie couldn't stop shaking. No dress rehearsal this time. This was it.

When Kenny was ready, they wordlessly held each other until the very last minute. He tore himself away, and she heard his footsteps on the stairs.

CHAPTER FOUR

O God, keep him safe.

Not until she watched him cross the street, did she break into terrible racking sobs and burrow her face into his pillow.

Somehow, she managed to dress and head out for her day of work. On the streetcar, she turned her face to the window, praying she wouldn't cry until she was in the washroom at work.

At California and Armitage, she got off the streetcar and walked, head down, toward the factory. But even though her eyes were on the sidewalk, she was aware of a group of people up ahead. One glance confirmed her fears. A number of men were standing in front of the draft board.

Kenny saw her coming and now he was coming to meet her. Once again they clung to each other, and she struggled to choke back the sobs. She knew the other guys were watching, and not wanting to cause him any embarrassment, she tore herself away and stumbled down the sidewalk to the factory.

Through blinding tears she found her way to the elevator, down the dim corridors, and to the washroom. She automatically pulled off her sweater and skirt and donned the ugly, navy blue, wrap-around work apron.

Somewhere on the way to her machines, she felt Margie's arms around her, and all her choked-back sobs came out on Margie's shoulder. "Come home with me tonight," Margie said, "And stay the weekend."

Jeanie nodded and blew her nose. "I won't be very good company, I'm afraid."

Margie handed her another tissue. "You're always good company," she said and then hurried to her machines.

Her work required little concentration, and Jeanie found herself reliving the morning's painful parting scenes over and over in her mind until noon.

33

Pat, though not as openly affectionate as Marge, was sympathetic, and several of the older ladies came over during the day to hug Jeanie or awkwardly pat her shoulder. Henry, her boss, pretended not to notice her red eyes.

After work she went home to pack some things for her weekend at Margie's.

When she opened the door, there were Kenny's work shoes just where he had taken them off. She cried as she stored them in the closet. Then, when she grabbed a towel to dry her tears, she smelled his after-shave lotion and cried even harder.

Before leaving for Margie's, she went downstairs to tell the Rassmussens where she was going. One look into their kindly eyes told her they had heard her sobs and were sharing her pain.

She gave them Margie's address, but she was not sure why.

"He'll be all right," the old man assured her with a pat on her arm. "God will protect him."

Jeanie tried to smile her thanks.

She arrived at Margie and John's apartment in time to help Margie set the table for dinner.

The three of them did their best to make pleasant conversation, but Jeanie was glad when bedtime came and she was free to cry again.

The next morning, the realization that Kenny was gone sent that same horrid shock through her, but she was determined to be calm. Then she looked in the mirror and let out a cry that brought Marge running.

"Look at my face," she moaned. It had broken out in an ugly red rash.

"Oh, my goodness. Your arms, too." Margie exclaimed.

CHAPTER FOUR

"Maybe I've got scarlet fever or something. We could be quarantined for weeks. John's work! He's in vital war work!"

Margie chuckled. "Oh, I don't think the outcome of the war depends on John's job." She felt Jeanie's forehead. "You don't seem to have a fever. Do you feel all right?"

"No I don't feel all right," Jeanie whimpered, "but I don't think I'm sick."

Thank goodness John and Margie had a car so people would not be staring at her on a streetcar on the way to the doctor.

A grandfatherly doctor peered at her throat and her eyes and said, "Have you had any emotional upsets recently?"

Gulping back sobs, Jeanie told him about Kenny's going into service the day before.

He nodded and patted her hand. "Don't worry. You'll be all right. Go home and get a good night's sleep."

By dinnertime the rash had almost disappeared.

They were still at the table when someone knocked on the door. "Jeanie!" John called. "Someone wants to see you."

"Who on earth?" she wondered aloud. No one but the Rasmussens knew where she was.

From the kitchen she could not see the door, and countless questions flashed through her mind as she crossed the living room.

"Kenny!" There he stood in full uniform.

"I got a weekend pass," he explained after several joyful kisses.

When Jeanie collected her wits enough to gather her belongings, John drove them home.

Only the knowledge that they would have to say goodbye again the next day marred their joy.

35

As Long as I Have You

They talked far into the night, not caring when they went to sleep or when they would get up in the morning.

It was a day unlike any other. No chores to do, no place to go. Only time to absorb each other's presence, while keenly aware that each tick of the clock brought them closer to another painful parting.

Once, Jeanie dozed as they lay cuddled close on the hide-a-bed. When she roused, Kenny was staring at her the same way she had stared at him days before, trying to memorize every detail of his dear face.

He ran his fingertips down her cheek, traced her lips, and smoothed her eyebrows. He had never done that before.

"I love it when you touch my face," she whispered.

At times, neither of them spoke. It was enough simply to be close.

It was their custom, before they went to sleep each night, to read from a little devotional book. Even though it was afternoon, she felt the need for comforting words. She handed the book to Kenny.

"You read," Kenny said.

Before she began to read, she told him, "I packed one just like this for you, you know. Will you try to read it every night?"

"I'll try," he promised.

After she finished reading, Jeanie wished they could pray together, out loud, but they lay quietly, each praying their own way.

Jeanie wondered if God seemed as far away to Kenny as He did to her. Surely, through the days ahead He would feel closer. If only she could pray all the time like Gram did. She remembered how she would cover her ears when Gram

36

whispered those long bedtime prayers. Not being able to hear, Gram had no idea how loudly she whispered.

Maybe I should have listened and learned how, Jeanie thought.

Her prayers were brief these days: *Keep Kenny safe. Help me get through today. Let the war end soon.* She never prayed that the Allies would win—how could God let Hitler win?

"I'm gonna need a good, clear picture of you," Kenny said as he gazed at her over soup and sandwiches that evening. Have one taken at a studio."

"But won't that cost a lot of money?"

"I don't care." He grinned and winked. "Wait'll those guys get a load of my baby."

Two more hours.

Cuddled on the bed again, Jeanie toyed with his bright new dog tags. "Why two?" she asked him.

"One stays with the body; one is sent home."

She shuddered. "Oh, what a thing to say!"

"You asked."

"Do you ever think about dying? Are you scared?"

"Yeah. I've thought about it and I'm scared. I don't want to die yet." He pulled her closer. "But I know where I'm going whenever I do."

Jeanie fought back her tears. She was determined not to cry until he had gone.

He kissed her tenderly over and over.

Once, as they caught their breath, she said, "I used to write the number of kisses on a calendar when we first started going out, but pretty soon I was writing things like, 'Couldn't count 'em or 'A zillion or so.'"

"Remember how we used to sneak at least one kiss a day the last year I was in high school?"

37

"Uh-huh. The best part was not knowing when it was coming. You had all sorts of tricks."

"Oh, Baby. Will we have a lot of catching up to do when I get back!"

When I get back. She would try to remember those words. Less than an hour now.

"Remember how we used to say that after we were married we'd never have to say good-bye?" Jeanie whispered.

"You used to say that."

He was right. She had wanted to believe the war would be over before he was drafted, but it was as if he always knew this day would come.

Her throat ached unbearably. She slipped away to the bathroom and allowed a few sobs to escape, hoping the noise of the flushed toilet would drown them out.

He was putting on his unfamiliar, new uniform when she came out. The sight of it set her trembling. "Do you want anything to eat?"

He shook his head.

"At least I get to ride the el train free—streetcars, too. I'll probably meet a lot of guys on the train going back to Camp Grant."

For a moment she envied all his new experiences and the busy life he would lead. All she could see ahead of her were big, black, noisy, smelly machines and long, lonely nights.

They did not say the word *good-bye.* He simply released her, turned and winked at the doorway, and walked out. Again.

Gasping to hold back the sobs, she ran to the front window and watched him cut across the street. He didn't look back.

CHAPTER FOUR

Tears streaming, she waited until she heard the el train pull away and its rumble blend with other city sounds. Then she let the sobs come.

I'm never going to stop, she thought in panic.

It was dark when she opened her eyes and the clock read 8:20. There was only one thing she had to do: it was Sunday night; she had to write to Gram.

"Oh, Mama," she wrote. "He's gone again. I just want to die." She crumpled the paper and began again.

Oh, Mama,

It seems like the future is as black as one of those nights when the clouds are so heavy not even the brightest star can shine through. Remember the time the flashlight bulb burned out when I was coming back from the outhouse? I couldn't see a thing. I bumped into the woodpile, and I think I would have stayed there until dawn, but a I heard a car rumble across the iron bridge and waited until the lights beamed over the hilltop. Boy! Did I run to the house while I could see.

I feel like I'm out in that kind of darkness right now. I can't see ahead and I don't have any idea when dawn will come.

She tore that one up too.

"Dear Gram," she wrote a third time.

"Guess what? Kenny left Friday, but he got a weekend pass . . ."

She wrote about how she went to Margie's house, how she broke out in a rash, how Kenny surprised her, and more.

That night she slept, hugging Kenny's pillow—his very damp pillow.

39

Monday evening, too tired and sad to do any housework, yet too wide awake to sleep, Jeanie lay in bed staring at the ceiling. Only one pinpoint of light appeared in her black sky that day. Margie reminded her that she would soon get a letter from Kenny, and then she would know where he would be taking his basic training. Maybe it would help a bit to be able to think of him in some specific place, instead of just out there somewhere.

That night, somewhere between sleep and consciousness, Jeanie found herself in a world of whirling white and stinging pain—like walking home from school in a blizzard. She had no idea how far from home she was. The high snowbanks from previous plowings kept her on the road, but she could see only a few feet ahead. Her fingers, toes, and face stung with cold, and the wind felt like an icy spear down her throat. But on and on she trudged, putting one foot in front of the other, over and over again, because there was no alternative. Enclosed in a white world of struggle and pain, she endured, knowing that each step brought her closer to home and relief.

It was like that for her now—not knowing how far away she was from the end of her separation from Kenny. Again, she would simply have to put one foot ahead of the other, day after day after day.

The sharp edge of Emma's pain over the news that Kenny would be inducted into the army had just begun to dull when Jeanie's next letter came, written the Sunday night Kenny left.

CHAPTER FOUR

Emma read it several times before she went back to sewing narrow, many-colored strips of material together for a rag rug. *Poor little girl.* She could picture Jeanie coming home to their empty little apartment, night after night. But there were many, many young wives doing the same thing, Emma reminded herself. *If only this terrible war would end soon.*

Each day, she read the *Milwaukee Journal* and tried to make some sense out of it. All those unfamiliar names. She had never even heard of Casablanca, where President Roosevelt and Prime Minister Churchill met in January. *What did they decide,* she wondered, *that would bring this war to an early end?* Anyway, this General Eisenhower, chosen to head the European operations, sounded like a good man. She reminded herself to pray for him every day.

But right here, right now, she hurt for Jeanie. More times than she could imagine, she hurt for one of her children—or for a whole family—and then had to work her way back to the Lord's peace and the joy of knowing that He was in control. Surely, by now, she should have that process down pat. Not so. Each time, she hurt as if she were the one in the painful situation. She knew so well all the kinds hurts and felt them all.

But hurting with them—for them—was not enough. She could be of no help to them if she simply felt sorry for them. She must deal with the fears that accompanied the hurts and get back to where she could surrender the whole thing to the Lord.

But that step sometimes took days.

It was a matter of going back to His Word, much of which came to her in hymns, and of believing what she knew to be true about God and what He had promised, rather than thinking about the problem.

"Oh, what peace we often forfeit, oh what needless pain we bear. All because we do not carry everything to God in prayer," she sang softly.

O Lord, she prayed, *I want to let you take over this worry, this ache for Jeanie. Help me.*

She sewed a bright red strip to a blue one that once was Jeanie's skirt. She remembered her wearing it—leaning close to the mirror by the washstand. Back then a new pimple was the end of the world for Jeanie. How far she has come since then. Emma saw that by the way she took the many disappointments at the time of her wedding.

Yes, Jeanie has grown stronger, and will grow stronger yet through this new trial. Ah yes, she reminded herself, *God's purpose is not to give us a comfortable life, but to make us become more like Jesus. I have to let her hurt or she won't grow.* She gave a wry little laugh, *How ridiculous.* As if she could do anything to prevent it.

"Ask the Savior to help you, comfort, strengthen and keep you. He is willing to aid you. He will carry you through," she sang. *O Lord, you will carry Jeanie through.*

Emma put her sewing aside. She must write to Jeanie.

Friday evening Jeanie eagerly opened Emma's letter. She wrote that she was sorry they had to be parted, sorry any young couple had to be parted. "The Lord will help you. Keep praying," she urged. After she had written a few other things about what was happening at home, she closed, as she always did, with "Mutch love, Mother." Below that she wrote, "PS: Keep busy. It helps."

CHAPTER FOUR

Jeanie smiled at the misspelled *much*. She often thought of correcting Gram but never did because she knew it would embarrass her.

Saturday morning Jeanie slept as long as she could to avoid the sad, lonely hours ahead.

That afternoon, she walked up North Avenue to the dime store at Crawford to buy a service flag for her front window. There were flags with one, two, and three blue stars and some with a gold star. She felt a cold chill run up her spine. Some of the flags had fringes, others were plain taffeta. She bought a plain one. After all, it won't hang there very long.

She bought a Hershey bar and enjoyed it as she walked home.

She was getting ready for bed when she heard a radio announcer tell that British Mosquito Bombers had raided Berlin in daylight. She was not sure what it all meant, but it sounded like progress.

At work Monday, Margie and Pat kindly did not ask if she had heard from Kenny. Surely there will be a letter tonight. He had been gone for over a week.

Coming home that evening, Jeanie could see the mailbox, which hung on the side of the house, as soon as she rounded the corner. There were little holes in it, and when there was mail those holes were white. Tonight they were dark.

Tuesday night she could see white showing through those holes. It was a postcard from Kenny. She read it as she walked slowly up the stairs.

Dearest Jeanie,
We left Wed. from Chicago. I'm writing on the train now. We went through Indiana, Kentucky, Tenn., Miss., and

43

now we're in Alabama. It's Thurs. We think we're going
back to Miss. I'm feeling swell.
Love and kisses, Kenny

She read it again when she was in the house. Mississippi. That seemed like another planet.

I'm feeling swell.

She let out a little sob of indignation. How could he feel
swell when she was dying of loneliness! It wasn't until bedtime that she felt happy that Kenny was feeling good.

Wednesday night she could see white through the mailbox holes again and she ran across the street. A letter. She
ran upstairs and didn't even take her coat off before she ripped
the letter open. Written in pencil, it was difficult to read.

Well, I ended up in the Army Air Corps. I'm in the Quartermaster Corps, but I could still get switched yet. We're
at Keesler Field, Miss. Now you can write.

He wrote some details about the forty-five hour trip and
said they were in little huts—fifteen guys to a hut. Basic training would be five weeks, and then he would be shipped somewhere for more training before he would be sent overseas.

Overseas! Mississippi was bad enough.

He said he was with a great bunch of guys and was having lots of fun. That word stung her. *Fun.* How could he be
having fun.

She fought back tears. Then she read,

I miss you, Darling. Oh, how I wish this war was over so
we could all live peacefully again. I love you more than
ever.

CHAPTER FOUR

She reread those words several times before she opened a can of tomato soup. Would she ever have fun—or even smile—while he was gone, she wondered.

There was another letter Thursday. He wrote that they would have to learn in twenty-eight days what generally takes thirteen weeks, so they would be working seven days a week. He was getting shots, marching in the hot sun, getting up at 4:30. It didn't sound like fun anymore.

When Jeanie stopped at Vi and Art's after church Sunday, she told all that Kenny had written. Vi said she didn't mind if she didn't get many letters from him, but she hoped he was writing to the folks.

Jeanie stopped at the corner drugstore on her way home and bought a Hershey bar.

He's been gone two weeks, she thought as she laid out her clothes for work the next day. Right now, she could not see a speck of light in the dark sky, and the ache deep inside her ceased only when she slept.

But even painless sleep was rare, because she often dreamed that Kenny was right there beside her. And when she awoke, the shock of finding herself alone made her whimper like a beaten pup. *Oh, please, God,* she prayed that night in bed. *Let me see just a little light.*

She waited and waited as tears slid down her cheeks into the pillow. Two whole weeks since he had been beside her. They seemed like two years.

Then a light-bringing thought came, *We are two weeks closer to the end of the war.*

"Thank you!" she murmured . . . and slept.

45

Time had become Jeanie's enemy. She wished it was possible to make a huge pleat in it, so that the present moment merged with the moment of Kenny's return.

The term *killing time* suddenly made sense. Time—filled with longings so deep they crowded out all other thoughts and feelings—needed to be eliminated. But how? She was grateful that her work at the factory took up a good portion of the day.

Of course Kenny's letters helped pass more moments painlessly. Besides, his letters gave her news to share with the girls at lunch, such as he had met a fellow from Chicago named Andy and they had become good buddies.

The girls thought it was good that Kenny had a buddy. If only they could stay together.

When she told them about the size of the camp, Margie and Pat were amazed. Kenny had written that when he was on KP one day, they served over twelve hundred men breakfast and over fifteen hundred lunch, and that kitchen was only one of thirty in the camp. He got to run the "china clipper" dishwasher that day.

But after several days of talking about what Kenny was doing, one day Margie slipped her arm around Jeanie's shoulders as they walked back to their machines. "Jeanie, we like knowing about what Kenny writes, but when are you going to stop living his life and start living your own?"

Jeanie stared at her in amazement. She wasn't aware of what she was doing. That evening she realized Margie was right. Her life was nothing but work, letter writing, a little housework, and lunchtime talks with the girls. Yes, she stopped over at Vi and Art's now and then, but she had no friends outside of work. At church, people sometimes nodded and smiled at her, but she didn't know anyone by name.

That night she thought about how she could find friends, go places, do things. She knew a girl named Gen, who had spent her summers in Wisconsin before she started to work. She now lived in Chicago year round. Once, she and Kenny had even double-dated with Gen and her boyfriend, Warren, when he had come up from Chicago. She decided to phone her sometime to see if they might get together. Sometime. She wasn't ready yet. It was easier to curl up in the rocker and remember how it was when Kenny's laughter rang throughout the small rooms, when she was so often in his arms, when her forehead rested against his neck and she could feel his pulse. . . .

But her striving to fill that awful void by trying to remember just how it used to be, left her frustrated and exhausted. It was always beyond her reach, and she would sob until there were no more tears.

That week when she went downstairs to pay the rent, the old lady answered the door. Jeanie was shocked to see

CHAPTER FIVE

how frail she was. As Gram would say, "A stiff breeze would blow her away."

"Oh, come in. Come in." Mrs. Rasmussen urged, and when Jeanie hesitated, she clutched her elbow with surprising strength and drew her into the cozy little kitchen.

Mr. Rassmussen hastily put aside his newspaper, beamed a smile, and invited her to sit down.

"You'll have some tea," the old lady said. It was a statement, not a question. "The kettle's hot."

"Well, now, how is the young man doing? Where is he?" the old man asked, leaning across the table so he would not miss a word.

"He's at Keesler Field, Mississippi," Jeanie said. "In the air corps."

The old man's eyebrows went up, and Jeanie quickly explained that Kenny was in the quartermaster corps, not learning to be a pilot, navigator, or bombardier. "He thinks he might be going to truck driving-school after his five weeks of basic training."

The old lady looked questioningly at her husband.

He nodded. "That's good! He may be close to the war but not right in it."

"That's just what he wrote. I'm glad he isn't in the infantry like his brother, Ray."

She jabbered on to her eager audience. "One time he wrote that he had just got back from chow, and they had ham, potatoes, string beans, Jell-O, noodles, and toast all slopped together in a mess kit. He said he used to wonder why they called them mess kits. Now he knows."

It took just a moment for the old lady to catch the pun, but then she laughed heartily.

How blue her lips are, Jeanie thought.

49

As Jeanie sipped tea from a thin china cup and nibbled at a piece of fruitcake, she learned that the Rasmussens attended a little church a few blocks away of the same denomination as the one Jeanie attended, but a different synod. When they invited her to come, she explained that she had already joined the church that her sister-in-law and family attended.

"Your grandmother? She is well?" the old man asked.

"Oh, yes. She'll soon be seventy-four. She has a lot of arthritis, but otherwise she's fine. She had a heart attack when she was in her sixties, but she got over that and started walking the two miles again to visit my Aunt Ella. There are some steep hills, too. She's almost deaf, though. That's why I talk so loudly," Jeanie chuckled. "I'm so used to shouting at Gram that whenever I see someone with gray hair, I start hollering."

The old man smiled. "Well, we don't hear that well either—especially in a crowd."

Jeanie told them about Gram's thirteen children, her over forty grandchildren, and a growing number of great-grandchildren.

"We were never blessed with children," the old lady said softly, her eyes on her teacup.

"Not many relatives left when you get to be our age," the old man said. "I have a cousin a few blocks from here and a nephew in De Kalb—that's all. Oh, we have some friends at church, but the old friends are all gone."

He abruptly began to talk about the war, as if eager to change the topic of conversation. He jabbed the newspaper headline with a knobby finger. Jeanie read: US AND FRENCH TROOPS FORCED BACK IN TUNISIA. She didn't even know where Tunisia was. She made a mental note to buy an atlas.

CHAPTER FIVE

The old lady's eyelids looked heavy, and once her head nodded. "I have to go," Jeanie said. "Thank you so much."

They urged to her stop in anytime, but to certainly plan to stay longer next week when she came to pay the rent.

When Jeanie wrote to Kenny that night, she described the visit in detail. "It gives me a nice, secure feeling to know they are down there. What a dear couple. Imagine being married fifty-three years!

Another speck of light in the dark sky, she thought before she went to sleep.

At work Friday, some ladies groaned when Henry, the foreman, announced they would be working most Saturdays from now on. But Jeanie was delighted. One thing she intended to do while Kenny was gone was to save money.

On her way home from work Saturday night, she stopped at a dime store and bought an atlas. "Follow the Global War on These Global Maps," it read on the cover. That evening she spent almost an hour studying maps and earlier military actions. Oh, they were complicated—arrows all over the place—especially the Pacific war zone.

One map, filled with lines showing transportation arteries, helped her understand why Tunisia was important. She didn't know that North Africa was so close to Spain. Now she could see that it was a vital sea route to southern Europe. Once, she heard a man on a streetcar say that the allied troops would probably invade Italy and almost everyone was waiting for an invasion of France from England. She leaned back and closed her eyes, imagining the Italian and German forces caught between the Allied army coming up from the south, invading from the west, and the Russians bearing down on them from the east. How long before this would happen? Where would Kenny fit in the picture? What about that complicated war in the Pacific?

51

Maps swam before her eyes that night in bed. This war was far beyond her understanding, but at least it took her mind off of her aching and emptiness.

That struggling-through-a-blizzard feeling was with her day after day. There was little to life but going to bed, getting up, going to work, eating, sleeping, going to bed . . . one foot ahead of the other, over and over again.

She had that struggling-through-a-blizzard feeling on her way home from work Wednesday evening, February 24. She had been home only a few minutes when there was a knock on her door.

The old man stood white-faced on the second stair, his chest heaving. He hoisted himself up the last stair and leaned his gaunt frame against the doorway.

Jeanie could see by his ashen face that something terrible had happened.

"My wife, . . . she's gone! She went in her sleep last night."

Jeanie gasped. "Oh, no!"

She took his arm and motioned to a chair. He sat down heavily and stared at the table. "She's gone. She's gone," he kept saying, as if trying to convince himself it was true.

Jeanie sat down and laid her hand on his. She could feel it trembling.

"At least she went peacefully. No suffering," he said.

"Yes," Jeanie murmured. She couldn't think of anything to say to comfort him.

He looked up at her. "You will come to the funeral home tomorrow after work?"

Jeanie nodded.

"I don't expect you to come to the funeral. You have work."

Chapter Five

He gave her the address of the funeral home, then scraped his chair back and got to his feet. "I will see you tomorrow," he said and went slowly back down the stairs.

For a few moments Jeanie paced the floor and then threw herself on her bed and sobbed. *Poor old man.* That night, life held new meaning for Jeanie as she realized how suddenly it could end. Somehow, she had to find a way to make hers meaningful, not simply plod along through it each day.

As usual, she cried before she went to sleep, but tonight her tears were not only for herself and Kenny.

Looking down at the little lady in her casket the next day, Jeanie caught a glimpse of the young woman she once was. Maybe because gravity no longer exerted its distorting force, she looked years younger.

"She was beautiful," the old man said.

"Yes, I can see she was," Jeanie said softly.

She squeezed his hand, still not knowing what to say. She sat on a stiff chair for a while with a group of murmuring people, and then she went home to the empty house.

At work the next day, Margie asked, "Aren't you afraid to stay there? He's so old. What if he dies too? What would you do?"

A chill raced through Jeanie. She stammered, "I . . . I don't know."

"You'd better start thinking about moving," Pat said.

"We're pretty sure John will get another notice to report for induction soon," Margie said, "and he probably won't get a deferment this time. You could move in with me, if you don't mind sleeping on the sofa."

That evening, Jeanie poured out her fears in her letter to Kenny, but she still couldn't fall asleep for a long while.

53

How could she leave these memory-filled rooms? She could see Kenny everywhere. To others it was only a grubby, little, furnished apartment in an ancient house, but to her it was home—their home.

Still, what if something did happen to the old man? What if she found him dead one day? She shuddered. What would happen to the house? Would she be forced to move in a hurry?

Questions swirled far into the night.

Sunday morning, Mr. Rassmussen came up and asked her to help him with his top shirt button and cuff buttons. "She always did it for me," he said sadly.

Jeanie told him to let her know if there was anything else she could do, and he promised he would.

At work, the girls again asked about her plans. When she went down to pay the rent she told Mr. Rasmussen, "I may be moving in with a girlfriend . . . if her husband goes in service."

The old man looked as if she had struck him. He reached for the back of a chair for support. "You can't leave me!" His voice broke. "You're all I've got!"

Jeanie was so shocked that later she couldn't remember a thing she had said. To her Mr. Rasmussen was just her landlord. But to him, she was all he had.

"Mama, what should I do?" she wrote to Gram. Oh, if only she could talk to Gram. She always knew the right thing to do.

Sunday morning when she again helped Mr. Rassmussen with his buttons, he told her he would soon sell the house. "But I will find good people who will let you stay. Don't move."

Jeanie nodded and tried to smile.

CHAPTER FIVE

"I was wondering," he said, "would you like to buy her sewing machine? You said you like to sew."

"Oh yes, I love to sew. Could I see it?"

It was a small treadle machine with a drop head—not a box-on-top like Gram's. The cabinet top looked like new when the old man lifted the scarf that covered it.

"I think it runs all right. She didn't use it much these last years."

Jeanie sat down and sewed a scrap of cloth the old man had found for her. The machine ran smoothly and quietly. It didn't skip any stitches.

"How much will you sell it for?" she asked. She was afraid he might want fifty dollars, since it might be worth something as an antique.

"I was thinking ten dollars," he said. "Is that too much?"

"Oh no. That would be fine." she answered hastily, and that afternoon Jeanie had her very own sewing machine. For the first time since Kenny left, she had something to be excited about.

Wednesday evening, Jeanie tore open Kenny's letter. He wrote that he and Andy had gone to see the movie, *Random Harvest.*

It was the best I've ever seen. Darling, I was so homesick for you, I darn near cried. Then I came back to the hut and I got your letter about the old lady dying, and I did cry. It makes me feel so helpless. I can't do a thing but pray that you'll be OK You won't have to move, will you? If you can, keep our place, but I don't know what to tell you to do.

The rest of his letter was filled with loving words—how he missed her, how he longed to be home with her—but

55

As Long as I Have You

ended with a note of confidence. "I know you'll be OK, because you are the type of woman who can take it."

Sometime during the night Jeanie woke up and knew one thing, she would not move. This was their home, and she would keep it until Kenny came home. She wondered why she had even considered moving.

Gram wrote the same thing, "Oh, don't move unless you just have to. That little place is your place."

When she announced her decision to Margie and Pat, they told her they hoped it would all work out for her, and the subject was closed.

At the Crawford department store, Jeanie bought pale yellow cotton material with a herringbone weave and a pattern for a blouse. She couldn't wait to try her new machine. She bought a quarter of a pound of chocolate covered peanuts, too.

It was like living again to cut and sew. The little machine purred. It was after midnight when Jeanie looked at the clock. The bag of candy was empty, and the blouse was ready for hand sewing.

Rationing hadn't bothered Jeanie a great deal, but when she found the sugar canister empty and then couldn't find her ration book, she was more than bothered. For two days she hunted and hunted. No ration book. What would it take to get another one?

Then a bulky letter came from Kenny with an air mail stamp on it. Because he could mail letters free, he never used air mail. She couldn't wait to open it.

The ration book! He had found it in the devotional book she had sent with him.

"I hang my head in shame," he wrote. (A favorite line of his in high school.) "I have to confess that I haven't been

56

CHAPTER FIVE

reading the devotional book, or I would have found your ration book. Guess you hadn't missed it, or maybe you just didn't think to tell me."

It was good to have sugar for her Wheaties again. Good, too, to know that Kenny had promised to read a little in that book every night.

A few days later he wrote, "Guess what? Andy's wife lives only a couple blocks from you. Andy says she's lonesome too. Why don't you call her?"

He included her phone number and the address, and Jeanie was surprised to see that she lived only about three blocks away. Her name was Lu.

Nervously, Jeanie phoned from the corner drug store. Lu's mother answered and called her. Lu had a squeaky little voice that made Jeanie a bit uncomfortable, but she seemed very friendly. "Come on over." she urged. "I've heard so much about you from Andy. Sounds like that man of yours thinks you're just about perfect." She giggled an odd little giggle.

"Oh, Jeanie!" Lu squealed when she opened the door. "I'm so glad you came. I can't wait to hear all about you two."

Lu was a tiny blond with a little-girl face that matched her voice.

Lu's parents graciously welcomed Jeanie, and the girls spent most of the evening lounging on Lu's bed, talking and giggling. Jeanie found herself quite at ease telling all about her and Kenny's high school romance and their wedding.

But when Lu showed her their wedding photographs, Jeanie was stunned. She had never seen such splendor. Lu wore a magnificent diamond next to her diamond-encrusted wedding band. A sharp contrast to Jeanie's narrow band with its chip diamonds.

Walking home, Jeanie pondered what to tell Kenny. Anything she wrote, he would probably share with Andy. While she had had a pleasant time, she had been sorely aware of vast differences in the way they saw life. Lu liked things—expensive things. She had been to the opera, the ballet, the theater—things Jeanie knew nothing about.

She wrote a safe letter, telling Kenny that she and Lu would probably get together now and then and that she was glad they lived so close to each other.

But at noon the next day, she talked more freely with Pat and Margie. "I'm afraid to get into a friendship that might not work out, because the guys are such good friends."

Margie shrugged. "What do you have to lose? You may be different, but sometimes it's good to be with people who don't think exactly the way we do."

"You can always make excuses if she invites you and you don't want to go," Pat suggested.

Jeanie groaned. "I'll have to invite her over. I wonder what she'll think about our shabby little rooms?"

A few days later as Jeanie waited for Lu, she was even more nervous than she had been when she went to Lu's house. She scrubbed and waxed the scarred linoleum floor, polished the black, painted table by the front window and the two wooden rockers that were also painted black. The only furniture with original finish were the two dressers standing side by side behind the door. A spotless, white tablecloth with hand-embroidered yellow daisies covered the old, wooden kitchen table.

"Oh . . . cozy," Lu said, after looking around. "You've been here how long?"

CHAPTER FIVE

"Since September."

"You don't have parents here, do you?"

"No, my grandmother and Kenny's parents are in Wisconsin."

Lu plopped down on the hide-a-bed, which was made up to look like a sofa. "Oh, well. You can get a better place before long." She flipped back her blonde hair. "I told Andy I was not about to live in some little dump. We could just stay with my folks until we can get a nice place."

Jeanie had no time to reply, even if she had found words.

Lu gushed on. "I'm going to see Andy just as soon as he gets out of boot camp. You won't catch me sitting around here, keeping home fires burning. You do plan to go and see Kenny, don't you?"

Jeanie confessed she hadn't even considered the possibility.

Again, it was a chore to write something positive to Kenny that night.

"I sure hope you two get along as well as Andy and I do. He's sure a swell guy," Kenny had written.

Jeanie groaned and picked up her pen.

Several weeks later Kenny wrote, "Andy's wife really likes you. She said we have the ideal place for a couple. I'm so glad you two like each other."

"She said *that?*" Jeanie exclaimed out loud. She couldn't believe Lu had written that about their apartment—not after the way Lu had said, "Oh well. You can get a better place before long."

She read on. "Hey, don't bother to put a lipstick kiss on the back of my letters. The sarge kissed it before he threw it at me, and all the guys laughed.

59

"I heard today that about eight hundred guys washed out of cadet school," he continued. "Only about fifteen out of a hundred make it."

It really must be tough, she thought.

He told her they would soon go on a twenty-mile hike with full gear. She didn't envy him.

"I'm glad you don't plan to move," he wrote in the next letter. "It will work out. I'm praying nice people will buy the place."

March 7 he wrote, "This will be my last letter from Keesler Field. We're shipping out tomorrow. I'm sure glad to get out of here but sad because Andy isn't shipping with us. I sure hate to leave him behind."

Jeanie heaved a huge sigh.

"I'm feeling swell," he continued, "tougher than ever. No one better cross my path."

That didn't sound like the Kenny she knew. *Was he changing?*

She didn't get another letter until March 15. It was postmarked Fort Warren, Wyoming. He wrote, "Boy, where they don't send a guy. We're three miles from Cheyenne. Took us seventy-three hours to get out here. Man! You should see those mountains. There's so much I want to write, but I've got to do so much stuff before lights go out. I'll have to cut it short.

"The grub is swell, and we even get to eat off plates instead of mess kits and live in nice warm barracks. I start school Monday morning and have eight weeks before I get shipped out again."

The next day, March 16, the temperature went up to seventy-eight degrees. Jeanie took a kitchen chair out on the back porch and sat down with her feet up on the railing. A robin flew to a nearby branch. It was spring. The

CHAPTER FIVE

grass was still not very green, but a few more warm days would change that. It felt good to be outside, to have the gray winter behind her, but it hurt to think of enjoying spring alone.

A few evenings later, there was a knock on her door, and Mr. Rassmussen stood there with a young, smiling couple. "This is Mr. and Mrs. Pedersen. They want to look at the house."

Jeanie welcomed them, and the tall, young man with nice, soft eyes said, "This is Thelma, and I'm Charles."

Thelma wore her blond hair waved close to her head. Jeanie could see that she was pregnant. Jeanie nodded and smiled, and then the couple followed Mr. Rassmussen around the apartment.

Not long after they had gone, Jeanie heard footsteps on the stairs and opened the door before the old man even got to it.

"Well, do you think you'd like them?" he asked as he sat down at the table. "They would like to buy the house."

"Yes, . . . yes. They seem very nice," Jeanie answered. "But you don't have to ask me. It's your house."

He patted her hand. "I know, but you were here first. I want it to be good for you. They are a nice couple. We go to the same church."

She again assured him she thought they were pleasant people.

She couldn't wait to tell Kenny and Gram, but decided to wait until the sale was final.

Kenny continued to write about truck-driving school, which he seemed to be enjoying. He said he was learning how to tear down a motor and put it back together again— all sorts of new things.

61

Then one evening there was a different kind of envelope in Jeanie's mailbox. Her first allotment check.

The same evening Lu dropped in on Jeanie, apparently hoping to continue their friendship despite the fact that the army had separated their husbands. She, too, had received her first allotment check but was not nearly as excited about it as Jeanie.

"I'm not going to use a cent of it," Jeanie told her.

"I might save some of it too," said Lu, "after I pay off our wedding rings."

Jeanie was too shocked to answer. Imagine! Andy and Lu had been married seven whole months, and their rings still weren't paid for.

At work the next day, Jeanie received another kind of shock. As Margie had feared, her husband John lost his deferment and had to go in for his physical.

"But they turned him down," said Margie. "Classified him 4-F."

"Why?" Jeanie managed to ask.

"Because of his heart. We didn't even know there was anything wrong with his heart. The doctor has advised us to go back to Nebraska and lead a quiet life. He has been under a lot of strain at this job."

"When do you think you will be leaving?" Jeanie reluctantly asked. She couldn't bear the thought of Margie leaving.

"We think about the first of May."

That night she sadly wrote Kenny. "Margie and John will be leaving in a few weeks. Oh, I'm going to miss her."

When Jeanie came home from Art and Vi's on Sunday, she found a note from Lu. She wanted Jeanie to go along with her and her family to their summer cottage. Still hopeful of ending the unpleasant relationship, Jeanie was glad

CHAPTER FIVE

she had not been home. That hope was crushed when she read Kenny's very next letter.

"Can you believe it?" he wrote. "Andy's here! They got in Friday, but he didn't get a chance to look me up. We're in different regiments, but we can still get together now and then. I guess you just can't break up a good team."

Jeanie groaned. Lu would still be in her life.

She continued reading. "Maybe now I won't be so lonesome and blue if Andy and I can see each other. Man, a couple times I just wanted to go over the hill. I miss you so much I don't know what to do. I can't imagine how I'd stand this army if I didn't have you to come home to. As long as I have you, I can take most anything. I love you more every day, if that's possible."

Jeanie cried.

In his next letter Kenny wrote, "We just got done with our floor show—that's what we call scrubbing the floor.

"I have to take my shots over because they gave them too far apart at Keesler field. Only two more to go. Man, I'm so full of holes, I'm probably going to leak."

When Jeanie tried on her spring clothes, she got a big surprise. They were all too tight. No wonder! For weeks she had been eating candy bars and the girls had taken turns bringing sweet rolls to work for the morning break. When she got on the old scale at work, she found she had gained fifteen pounds. It was good-bye to all the candy bars and sweet rolls if she hoped to see Kenny's admiring glances.

"Oh, I'm so excited," she soon wrote to Kenny. "That young couple bought the house. They're moving in next week. The old man is going to live with his nephew in De Kalb. He has been so dear: I'll miss him. He gets up at

63

As Long as I Have You

about five to put coal in the furnace, so I'll be warm when I get up."

Yes, she would miss the old man. Often, he would be waiting at the back door when she came home, and she would stop to chat awhile. One time he looked searchingly at her and asked, "How are you?"

Jeanie answered brightly, "Oh, I'm all right."

He nodded and patted her arm. "I know. I hear you crying at night. I cry too."

She wanted to hug him. As she washed her face at bedtime that night, she realized old people had feelings too—even if they weren't young and madly in love.

If only she could find a way for time to go quickly. Sometimes she felt like a wind-up doll—empty on the inside, merely going through the motions of living.

She felt the same way the previous winter, when she was a senior in high school and Kenny was in Chicago, but then she knew when it would end. Now the end was nowhere in sight.

One morning when she was riding to work, still half asleep, part of a poem she learned in grade school came back to her. "Here hath been dawning another new day. Think, will thou let it slip useless away?"

Later, as she was at her machine, changing spools of gleaming white nylon cord, more of the poem came. "Out of eternity a new day is born. Into eternity at night will return."

The words spun around and around in her mind like a phonograph record with the needle stuck in one groove.

At noon she told Pat and Margie about the haunting poem. "I can't get it out of my mind. Have you ever had that happen?"

CHAPTER FIVE

"Not poetry, but sometimes I can't get a song out of my head," Margie said. "Do you remember it now?"

"Of course," Jeanie said, clearing her throat.

Here hath been dawning another new day.
Think, wilt thou let it slip useless away?
Out of eternity a new day is born.
Into eternity at night will return.

"I know there's more, but I can't remember," she sighed. "It's a poem I learned in grade school, but I don't have the faintest idea who wrote it."

Pat nodded. "That's something worth thinking about— that a day really is precious and it won't ever come again."

Jeanie scowled. "The days don't seem precious to me right now. I just want 'em to go by."

Margie tilted her head, as she often did, studying Jeanie's face. "You can't afford to waste these days, Jeanie. There's too much to learn and to do."

Jeanie folded her lunch bag and sighed. "Oh, I suppose so. I guess I could do more sewing. I have a sewing machine now."

Pat smiled. "Good girl. That's a good place to start."

Jeanie still was not enthusiastic. What good was doing anything without Kenny ?

But she did buy a pattern and some brown fabric for a skirt to wear with the yellow blouse she had recently sewn.

Each evening she sewed awhile, and on Friday she realized the week had gone by more swiftly.

"Keep busy," Gram had advised in a letter. That was it. No more killing time. She would think of more things to do, set goals, work until she was exhausted, and at bedtime ask herself what she had accomplished that day.

65

As Long as I Have You

Before she went to sleep that night, Jeanie got up twice to add items to her things-to-do list.

Six

Early in February, Jeanie wrote Gram that she planned to take a week off and come home at Easter time. But now, after one of Lu's drop-in visits, she was thinking of maybe visiting Kenny at Fort Warren, Wyoming. Lu said she was going to visit Andy—no matter what.

One minute Jeanie thought it was a good idea, and the next minute she was not sure at all. For, as much as she wanted to be with Kenny, it seemed terribly impractical to take a train to Denver, then catch a bus another hundred miles to Cheyenne, find a place to stay, and then be able to see the guys only on Sunday.

From Kenny's next letter, she knew his thoughts were much like her own. He wrote,

> Andy says Lu is coming out to see him and wondered if you are coming too. I told him I hadn't even thought about it, because the only day off I have is Sunday, and you never know when that can get screwed up. Gee,

honey, you know I want to see you, but I can't see making that long trip for just that little time together. He says the two of you could get a room and split the cost. But what I want to know is who gets the room on Sunday? I heard some guys talking in town one night, and one guy's wife had a heck of a time finding a place to stay. I can't get off to reserve a place for you ahead of time, so you would have to find one yourself. You know I want to see you! I don't want to tell you not to come, but I just don't know if it's the thing to do.

Jeanie read and reread his letter. Her head agreed it was impractical, but her heart ached for him. Then she would think of being with Lu two whole weeks and she would be more in favor of staying home. Lu planned to stay so she could be there two Sundays.

With her thoughts in such turmoil, Jeanie totally lost interest in sewing. At times the desire to be with Kenny was so overwhelming, she was willing to put up with any inconvenience—even being with Lu for two weeks. But then her practical nature would take over again, and she would think of all the reasons not to go.

Pat and Margie were of little help, except to listen to her recite the pros and cons day after day.

As she worked and thought hour after hour about how wonderful it would be to see Kenny, she convinced herself it would be worth any amount of time, money, and inconvenience for them to be together. But then Lu would come over, cracking her gum, talking nonsense in her silly little-girl voice, and Jeanie could not imagine living with her all that while.

Jeanie dreamed and struggled with the decision even in her sleep. She knew she had to make up her mind soon

CHAPTER SIX

and let Gram know if she would or would not be home for Easter.

One evening she tore open a letter from Kenny.

There's both measles and scarlet fever in our barracks, and we're confined to quarters until time to ship out to the next camp. That settles our ideas about you coming out. Andy's barracks is fine, so Lu is coming out. Oh, Baby, I want to see you so bad, but with the quarantine, it's impossible.

With mixed emotions, Jeanie folded his letter. It hurt to give up her dream of being with him, but she was relieved to have the decision taken out of her hands. She promptly wrote Gram that she would be home for Easter.

April 18, Kenny wrote on USO stationery with "Easter Greetings" at the top. He said he and a buddy named Bob had to make a trip to town so Bob could place a phone call to his wife. It was going to take three or four hours for the call to go through, so they were waiting in the USO.

He said the spring weather reminded him of when they were in high school and would take a walk every noon. "And remember the summer we were fifteen, when we walked the mile through the woods from your house to your Aunt Ella's? I never even kissed you! Boy, was I a fool."

Jeanie smiled, remembering those wonderful days when they were content to walk hand in hand and she felt like he was her best friend in the whole world. They had never run out of things to talk about.

Oh, Baby, I see couples together here in town and I'm so lonesome for you. I'd give most anything to be with you. But then I think of what torture it would have been to

69

sit in classes at the base, knowing you were right in town. I know it won't make up for not being able to come, but you can expect a little package. I'm sending three silver dollars—one for you, one for Joannie, and one for Kent.

Jeanie hugged the letter. They hadn't written about their children for a long time. For the past two years they talked about the children they would have—Kent and Joannie—and what they would be like. Kenny was sure Joannie would be just as sweet and loveable as Jeanie and that Kent would be the toughest kid in the neighborhood.

That evening, she had a happy time, dreaming about the four of them in a nice home of their own.

Taking the bus to Wisconsin was not such a good idea after all, Jeanie decided. She traveled over six hours and was not yet halfway home.

A pleasant young serviceman sat beside her for a few hours, and she would have enjoyed talking with him if she had not been so embarrassed by her short, red suit-skirt. It kept hiking up above her knees, and she had to keep pulling it down.

Then an old man, reeking of cigar smoke, took the soldier's place, and finally when she had about fifty miles to go, Jeanie was alone. Even so, she slept very little because the bus stopped so often.

It was good to be with the family again. Last Christmas, because her time with Kenny had been so precious, she had spent very little time with her cousins, who also lived

CHAPTER SIX

in the big, old farm house. She couldn't wait to see baby Gene, who had been born in November. When Jeanie had a baby in her arms, the rest of the world grew dim.

She wondered if three-year-old Arne could say "rug" now, instead of "nug" and if he would still want to help her make her bed in the morning.

Little brown-eyed Marie would say little but smile much, and ten-year-old tomboy Marilyn would probably spend more time in the barn than in the house.

Ron, five years younger than Jeanie, would stand by listening, ready to lend a hand wherever he was needed.

It would be fun to talk far into the night with Helen. (She had always prefaced her other aunts' names with *Aunt*, but her two youngest aunts were simply Helen and Olga.)

She doubted she would see much of Uncle Roy. He was so busy with farm work that he was rarely in the house.

And Gram. Would she still hover and fuss over every little thing? Jeanie tried to think of really important things to tell her because, as Gram continued to lose her hearing, conversation was becoming more and more difficult. Sometimes Jeanie had to resort to writing notes.

It was late morning when the bus stopped at the corner of Highway 13 and Highway 86 in Ogema, a block from Aunt Gertie's house. Sleepy, but excited, Jeanie got off and found both Gram and Aunt Gertie waiting.

"Just look at you!" Aunt Gertie exclaimed. "You look wonderful."

Gram hugged her hard and said, "My little girl! My little girl!" There were tears in her eyes when she released Jeanie.

"Here we thought you were pining away," Aunt Gertie said as they walked toward her house, "and you've gained

71

weight and look the picture of health. Turn around and walk backward so I can see you."

Laughing, they walked the rest of the way to Aunt Gertie's little yellow house—with Jeanie walking backwards.

They had time for lunch and a short visit before Roy came to take Jeanie and Gram home. A service flag with two stars—one for Clyde and another for Earl—hung in the front window. "I don't know what I'd do without Don," Aunt Gertie said. "Joe is gone so much, and I'm not used to being alone."

As soon as she said *alone* she dropped her usual light-hearted banter. She held Jeanie's eyes as she asked, "Is it getting any easier for you?"

Jeanie nodded and blinked hard.

Kenny timed his letters well. There was one waiting for her when they got to Gram's. He wrote that he planned to go to the Easter sunrise service and then to another service at nine.

He said that he received a letter from Margie. He was sorry to hear that they would be moving back to Nebraska, because he knew Jeanie would miss her. "She tells me you're gaining weight, but that you look great. Just don't keep on gaining. I don't want you to lose that twenty-four inch waist."

Jeanie glanced at the fragrant, freshly baked bread on Gram's table and sighed. It wouldn't be easy to keep the slim figure Kenny admired.

It felt good to sit in the familiar, old wooden rocker and listen to Gram tell about other family members. It was amazing that she knew so much when she heard so little. "Can't begin to keep track of where all the grandsons are stationed," she said without apology. "But I sure do pray for them."

CHAPTER SIX

How Jeanie wished Gram could hear the radio. What would she think if she could hear Edward R. Murrow's dramatic, "This . . . is London." She wondered if Gram even knew shortwave broadcasts could be heard several times a day, not only from London, but from the South Pacific as well. But even if she did know, there would be little sense in her listening, because the static challenged even those with keen hearing.

What progress, Jeanie thought. She recalled Gram telling that during the First World War, it was days, sometimes weeks, before news from the front reached the public by telegraph or newspaper.

Jeanie knew exactly what Gram would say if she could hear such a broadcast: "Oh my. What would Papa say?"

Each evening, as Jeanie chronicled the day's events to Kenny, she was aware of the contrast between life here on the farm and life in the noisy city.

> I couldn't believe that little church aisle was so short when I walked in on Easter morning. It seemed like a mile long when I walked it on our wedding day. It was so nice to see all those smiling faces at church. Back in Chicago I just walk in and out of church without talking to anyone, I wonder what Gram thinks about all during the service, since she can't hear what's going on. She had such a sweet expression on her face, I think she was probably worshiping the risen Lord more deeply than those of us who could hear.

She told him how she sat in church with her sister-like cousins, Grace and Ruby, without giggling even once.

As Long as I Have You

There isn't much to giggle about these days. Grace plans to be married soon and hopes to follow her husband as long as he's in the States. Chet, Ruby's boyfriend, has been in service over a year already. He's in North Africa. I miss Myrtle. Remember how she used to "mother hen" me in high school when I was a freshman and she was a senior? She and Harry are down in Seneca, Illinois. Harry is working in a shipyard on the Illinois River. They're building LSTs (I think that means "landing ship tanks"). Myrtle's brother, Harold, is down there too. (Remember, he married Grace Blomberg—the one with the gorgeous, red hair). Aunt Ella said I should try to get down to visit them sometime. The train from Chicago only takes an hour or so. Maybe I will.

'Helen let me bathe baby Gene this morning, and it was so much fun to see him splash and laugh," she wrote Monday. "I can't wait till we have our own baby."

Tuesday, the air was so soft one could almost grasp a handful of it. "Wanna go up by the stone piles and see if there are any mayflowers?" she asked little Marie. They ran across the snow-softened stubble field and leaped over the drainage ditch. "Do you kids dam it up like I used to?" she asked.

Marie nodded and pointed to the remains of a sad little dam. She soon found the first cluster of pale, lavender mayflowers, and they both crouched down to pick the long, downy stems.

"Do you know where the diamond rock is?" Jeanie asked her.

"Oh sure." Marie smiled and led the way to a rock of sparkling mica.

Jeanie laughed. "It's so small. I know the rock hasn't changed. I guess I have." Once these precious spots had been only hers. She never thought of the children who might have played there before her or would play there after her.

"I used to pretend it was made of real diamonds," Jeanie confided. "O Marie, I wonder how many city kids never get to pick a wildflower or smell earth in springtime, or dig little ditches to drain water?" But as they strolled back home, she thought of something worse across the ocean—*shells exploding and children hiding in fear, even on a beautiful spring day like this.*

That night she wrote Kenny about her walk with Marie. "We put the mayflowers in Gram's toothpick holder, just as I did when I was a little girl. Out in the fresh air and blue sky it's easy to forget that somewhere else guns are booming and bombs are falling."

Wednesday night Jeanie wrote,

> Your mother picked me up this afternoon. It took her week's gas ration, but she said she didn't need to drive around town. I stayed for dinner. I'd better not tell you about all the good food. Your dad seems fine—trouble with his eyes because of the sawdust, as usual. I love the way your mother puts drops in them and is concerned about his every need. I want to be that kind of a wife. I'll run your bathwater and lay out clean clothes if your work is the kind that you need to clean up when you get home. (Somehow I can't see you in a white-collar job.)

Jeanie nibbled the tip of her pen and thought back over the evening, sorting out what she would write and what she should leave out. She wasn't about to tell Kenny that his mother seemed more nervous than ever, anxious about both of her boys—especially Ray in the infantry. She wouldn't tell him about the delicious stuffed pork chops;

As Long as I Have You

applesauce; fluffy mashed potatoes; Jell-O salad; and four-inch high angel food cake. Nor would she tell him how she had been in agony because of his dad's noisy eating. She knew that all the years of working in a saw mill had taken a toll on his hearing and he couldn't hear himself. But knowing that didn't keep the chills from racing up her spine each time he took a loud slurp of coffee. She had to feign a trip to the outhouse just to get away from the table.

> But I have some big news. Vi's going to have another baby! I thought she seemed unusually tired, and one night when I got there to baby-sit, she said she didn't feel well and they were going to stay home. I didn't think too much of it. Of course your mother is having a fit because the first three are only a year apart, and when this baby comes, Billy will be only two. I can see Mother's concern for Vi, but it doesn't help Vi to have her so upset about it. But you know Mother! She always goes off like a rocket and then settles down and does everything she can to help. I guess Vi didn't want to tell me until she told Mother.

Thursday evening Gram and Jeanie ate with Roy, Helen, and the children, and Jeanie told about Kenny's plans to attend the Easter sunrise service.

Roy finished his last bite of potatoes and gravy, leaned back and laced his huge fingers across the front of his bib overalls as Jeanie went on. "He said there are usually about twenty to thirty thousand soldiers there, and the First Regiment band always plays just as the sun comes up."

Roy nodded and smiled. "That must be quite an experience—especially out there in the mountains."

76

Chapter Six

"Oh yes. He wants us to take a trip back there when he gets home. He really loves the mountains."

"Yeah, that would be nice," said Roy, "but it's going to take a while after this war is over to catch up with cars and tires and things like that. It'll take months for those big companies to retool to manufacture civilian goods again."

She wrote that to Kenny and added, "I won't mind waiting for trips and things. It'll be enough just to have you home."

There was so much Emma wanted to say to Jeanie these few precious days, but it was hard to know what was on the girl's mind. At least she could ask her questions that could be answered with a yes, no, a shrug, nod, or shake of the head.

So far a shrug told her that Jeanie was not thrilled with her work at the factory but that it was all right. A nod told her Jeanie had found a few new friends and was not quite as lonesome now, and another nod indicated that she visited Vi and her family quite often.

Jeanie wrote that she had bought the old lady's sewing machine.

"I'm so glad you have a sewing machine." Gram said, "That should keep you busy. It helps to be busy, you know."

What she really wanted to talk about was Jeanie's faith. But how could she just come out and ask, "Do you trust the Lord to protect Kenny?" She knew that Jeanie went to church every Sunday, but she also knew it took more than just going to church to have God's peace.

She studied Jeanie's face and the way she talked and moved. *Oh, dear,* she thought, *she still chews her lower lip and can't sit still a minute. If only she could learn to relax.*

Ah, but it was good to watch Jeanie take the white, ruffled curtains down from all four windows, wash them and let the breeze blow them dry. She washed the woodwork and windows, too. Then put the ironed curtains back up in a way that would please even Gertie, the family perfectionist.

Oh to be able to move so effortlessly again. She takes after me, Emma thought and smiled with satisfaction. *She takes pleasure in accomplishment, just like I do. Maybe I did teach her a few things.*

The one thing Emma was able to say before Jeanie left was, "Remember that time is precious. Make good use of these days."

When Jeanie smiled and nodded, Emma knew Jeanie was trying to do just that.

Seven

When Jeanie boarded the train on Sunday, she was glad she hadn't bought a round-trip ticket on the bus. She waved to Roy, stowed her luggage, and then sat sniffling almost all the way to Merrill.

She knew how lonely Gram would be back in her empty rooms. And now she had to face going back to her empty rooms.

And then she was back in Chicago, dragging her luggage through Union Station, up the escalator, and onto the el train. She was glad it was night and she didn't have to see the dingy clothes hanging on sagging lines from shabby porches; the torn window shades; the broken, patched windows; and milk bottles out on windowsills. It was depressing enough to hear the police sirens and the screech of the el brakes and to smell the city air so heavy with coal smoke and auto fumes. Maybe when Kenny got home they could get out of the city.

As Long as I Have You

There was mail in the box. Jeanie managed to get it and her luggage up the stairs without dropping anything. When she pulled the string for the ceiling light in the kitchen, there stood her landlord's little white refrigerator.

What on earth?

Torn between eagerness to read Kenny's two letters and finding out why the refrigerator was there, she settled for a quick scan of Kenny's love-filled letters. Then timidly she knocked on the door leading downstairs, knowing that the young couple had moved in while she was gone.

"Well, hello." Charles said cheerily. "We didn't know exactly when you'd be back. Come in."

"Just for a minute. I just got home and . . ." she pointed to the empty space in the kitchen where the refrigerator had stood. "How come?"

Thelma laughed, and Charles explained that when they bought the house, Mr. Rassmussen insisted she should have the refrigerator. Charles chuckled. "We promised we'd take good care of you. He's staying awhile with his cousin a few blocks from here, and we'll probably see quite a bit of him."

"But now you don't have a refrigerator. And I know how hard it is to get even a used one," Jeanie protested.

"Don't worry," Charles said waving away her concern. "We'll find one."

He asked where Kenny was stationed, and when Jeanie said he would be shipped out again soon, they both said they hoped he would be closer to Chicago.

Charles added that he had a brother, Kenneth, in service.

Jeanie had noticed earlier that Charles had a slight limp and presumed he was 4-F.

Back upstairs, Jeanie flipped through the rest of her mail. There was an envelope without a stamp that must have been

CHAPTER SEVEN

slipped into her mailbox. It looked like Margie's handwriting. She tore it open. It was, and she let out a little cry as she read that Margie and John had already left for Nebraska. She sagged down at the table and laid her head on her arm. Pretty Margie with the bubbly laugh was gone.

"I'm on an emotional roller coaster tonight," she wrote to Kenny the next evening. "I was depressed to be back in the ugly old city; happy to get your letters; surprised and delighted to see the refrigerator; glad to know that nice, young couple had moved in; and now I'm sad that I missed saying good-bye to Margie. Oh, how I'll miss her!"

At work the next day, Jeanie's eyes often filled with tears. She could picture Gram sitting alone, baby Gene laughing and cooing, the trees greening more each day, and then, in sharp contrast, her own lonely rooms. She tried to find something to look forward to, but all she could think of was the same old thing: get up, go to work, eat, sleep, and do it all over again. Her one hope was that Kenny would be moved closer to Chicago.

A few evenings later, there was gum-chewing Lu at her door.

"Boy, did you miss it," she squealed and flopped down at the table. "Did I have a great time in Cheyenne. Hey, you got a Coke?"

Jeanie shook her head. "How about a cup of tea?"

Lu wrinkled her nose. "Anyway," she said, leaning closer, "Andy got to come to town both Sundays and we kicked the other girls out for the whole afternoon. Whoo-ee!"

"Other girls?"

"Yeah, four of us got a room together. Two had to sleep on the floor, so we took turns with the bed."

"But what did you do during the week?"

81

Lu flipped back her blonde hair and studied her long, scarlet nails. "Well, we were always out till who-knows when, so we slept till nearly noon. Then we'd go down to a little coffee shop, and the lady there would let us work to pay for our lunch. I started out good with my money, but boy, did it go fast."

"What about dinner?"

Lu threw back her head and laughed. "I didn't buy one single dinner. There were always guys around who were more than glad to buy a girl dinner."

Jeanie gulped. "Guys?"

"Oh, for Pete's sake! You don't think I was going to hang around that dump all week, waiting for little Andy boy, do you?"

Jeanie stared at the table.

"Oh, don't look so shocked," said Lu in her squeaky little voice. "I didn't do anything really bad. All those guys want is to be with a girl."

Jeanie was speechless. Lu twittered on a while longer, and when she said she had to go, Jeanie was not about to argue.

She closed the door with a sigh. *Poor Andy!*

It took a long while to write to Kenny that night, because she had to be careful what she wrote. Even though Kenny would be shipped out soon, it was possible he and Andy might get back together again.

That night Jeanie dreamed all sorts of weird things.

In the morning her whole conversation with Lu seemed like a bad dream too. She shivered. What would she have done if she had found herself with those wives for two whole weeks?

CHAPTER SEVEN

But, even though she was faithfully working and waiting in her little home, for the next few days, a strange sense of guilt nagged her, as if she had forgotten to do something important. She couldn't think of anything she'd neglected to do. She always kept her apartment clean, paid the rent on time, and dutifully wrote to Kenny's parents and to Gram once a week, and Kenny every night.

She was about to tell Pat about the guilty feeling, when suddenly she knew why she was still plodding through the days without any purpose. The poem. It had helped her before. She let the words run through her mind, and when she got to the part "Think, wilt thou let it slip useless away?" she knew that somehow she had to make better use of her time until Kenny got back. She also knew she had been much too self-centered.

It felt good to know what was wrong. Now she had to do something about it.

At work the next day, as she changed tray after tray of spools, Jeanie made plans.

For one thing, she would try to help others. All during her childhood Jeanie had seen Gram's example. She would come home from a day of helping Ella or Olga, eyes sparkling and a new spring in her step. "I'm, tired," she would say, "but it's a good tired. I don't know what I'd do if I couldn't help others." Then she would tell about all the beans they had canned or all the mending she had done.

Vi could certainly use more help with a new baby coming. There was always ironing to do, and even though she couldn't iron as well as Vi did, she could press the children's play clothes.

By evening she had a mental list of how she could make better use of her time: (1) help Vi; (2) call Gen; (3) find a

83

As Long as I Have You

more difficult pattern and learn more about sewing; (4) buy *Woman's Day* magazine at the grocery store—it only cost a few cents; (5) learn more about being a good homemaker.

Another thing she needed to do was learn more about the city. She would visit museums and the art gallery on Lake Shore Drive. Before bedtime, she wondered how she could have allowed all these weeks to go by without doing anything other than her work at the factory and a little housework.

She resolved to ask herself every night if she had made the best use of that day. She vaguely recalled a scripture verse—something about redeeming time. She wasn't sure what all of it meant, but she knew that if something was to be redeemed, a price had to be paid. Chin in hand, she sat down to write to Kenny. She was willing to pay the price, to do whatever it would take to set these days free from waste. She smiled, thinking how proud Kenny would be of her when he got home.

Even wayward blades of grass growing along the brick buildings' walls were a welcome sight to Jeanie that spring of 1943. When three daffodils appeared right by the fence next door, she crouched down to get a better look at them. What a wonder they seemed after all those months of dead earth.

The old lady next door began appearing too. She reminded Jeanie of Gram, with her long skirts, cover-all aprons, and gray hair pulled straight back in a bun or "pug" as Gram called it. But she did not have Gram's sweet spirit. Jeanie had tried to talk with the old woman but found it almost impossible to understand her.

One Saturday, the woman's daughter told Jeanie that her mother spoke five different languages. Now Jeanie understood. The old lady obviously spoke them all at one time.

Was there no end to changes? One evening at Vi's, Jeanie learned that Art's mother felt unable to keep an apartment alone. Vi and Art badly needed a larger apartment anyway, so they decided to find one and have Art's mom move in with them.

They discovered an apartment just north of Fullerton Avenue on Bernard Street that would take three children and an expected fourth. Through the following weeks, Jeanie helped them pack, and one sunny Saturday the family moved out of their tiny Mozart Street apartment.

Though the new apartment was much larger and brighter and had three bedrooms, the children still ended up sleeping in the same room.

Kenny wrote that he had received the snapshots of her that she had taken in Wisconsin at Easter time, and he looked at them every chance he got. Of course he showed them to his buddies.

"They wonder how I ever got a girl like you," he teased, "and sometimes I wonder too." He went on with a whole paragraph of reasons why she was so special, and his assurances of love made Jeanie's heart glow.

Each evening when Jeanie got home from work, the first thing she did was turn on the radio to keep her company. Most of the news these days was about an Allied offensive in Tunisia. It sounded terribly complicated, but she prayed for a swift victory.

Kenny's May 11 letter told how they had gone on a bivouac up in the mountains, had run into a blizzard, and had spent the night in tents in the snow. He said he had woken up in the morning with his feet outside the tent in a snow bank. "I'm sure glad I slept with all my clothes—and my shoes—on."

To top off that day, he had pulled guard duty. "I found a big rock, built a fire on it, and sat there without any food. I couldn't leave my post, so I just waited and waited. I'd been

CHAPTER EIGHT

there over six hours when a couple guys came. They were all ready to leave and noticed I wasn't there to drive my truck. Was I starved! You can bet I hollered at 'em!"

Any day now he expected to be shipped out because the eight weeks of school were over.

On May 14, newspaper headlines screamed that the last Axis forces had surrendered to the Allies in Tunisia. Jeanie began to pray that the Allies would soon invade Sicily, which according to the map, seemed to be the logical spot to take before landing on the mainland of Italy.

No letters! Day after day, Jeanie's heart would leap if she saw white showing through the mailbox holes as she crossed the street. But always they were letters from someone else. Then Friday, May 21, there was a letter from Kenny.

"Santa Maria, California." she wailed. She'd hoped he would be stationed closer. Instead he was farther away.

Kenny wrote that he was in a "hell hole" of a camp and about as disgusted and disappointed as he could get. He had counted on being closer to home, here he was in this jungle.

His next letter was no better. "I thought it was bad when seven guys went AWOL at Fort Warren," he wrote. "Last night thirty-four men went over the hill. I don't blame them a bit. If I didn't have you, I probably would too. Now a couple guys have scarlet fever, so we can't leave the area. The only good part is we don't have to work. We're lying around in the sun all day."

Letter after letter had the same depressed tone. "I hurt deep down inside of me knowing we're so far apart. What I wouldn't give to have you in my arms for just five minutes. Maybe I'll feel better when our mail comes through. I haven't had a letter since we left Fort Warren."

87

"At least I'm in a company now and in a new unit," he wrote May 24. "We're sleeping in double bunks and I'm right up by the ceiling. It's so hot I hardly slept at all last night. I'm so darn disgusted. But Baby, as long as I have you, I can make it. I just wish our mail would get through."

He wrote on May 26 that he finally got a letter and it made him feel a hundred percent better. Evidently he still had a lot of letters coming because he wanted to know who Thelma was.

"I walked into a pretty good job," he wrote the next day. "I was picked to be the supply sergeant's assistant because I can type. That's the army for you. I just got my truck driver's license and here I am typing! His pay, he said, was $16.75 for the month after money was taken out for war bonds. "I can't go anywhere to spend money, and I can get a carton of cigarettes at the PX for about $1.30, so I'll manage."

He said he was getting to know some guys and having some fun, but that "nothing compares to those four months after we were married. They were the happiest four months of my life."

That sounded like Kenny again. For the first time in over a week, Jeanie felt better after reading his letter. What really made her happy was that he thought he would get a furlough when he got to the next camp.

June 10 he wrote that they would be shipping out in a day or two, and she shouldn't worry if she didn't hear from him for a while.

Then June 18 a letter came postmarked Pendleton, Oregon. He said he had been on a train four whole days. The camp was nice. They even had sheets on their bunks, but he heard they would be working from "can to can't"—from

CHAPTER EIGHT

the time they can see in the morning till they can't see at night.

Jeanie wrote, "I still haven't seen either Charles or Thelma when they weren't smiling. Thelma lets me use her vacuum cleaner whenever I want, and you should see how much brighter the front room carpet looks. That carpet sweeper wasn't much good. Did I tell you she's expecting a baby the end of June? Imagine it. A baby right here in this house. Am I glad I didn't move."

Saturday Jeanie was coming out of Pauli's supermarket when she met Lu. Weeks had passed and Jeanie had made no attempt to contact her. Andy shipped from Fort Warren to a camp near the Washington border.

Much to Jeanie's relief, Lu didn't suggest that they get together.

Kenny wrote June 20 that he missed her so much he didn't know what to do, and "I'd be the worst guy in this army if it wasn't for you. I've been in this army five months, and it seems like five years."

The big family news was that Kenny's brother Ray was accepted for officers training at Fort Benning, Georgia. His mother however, would have been a lot happier if he weren't in the infantry.

When Jeanie got home from work June 23, Charles met her at their back door. "He was absolutely beaming," Jeanie wrote to Kenny that night. "Elizabeth was born this morning. I can't wait to see her."

When Kenny wrote that he was quite sure he would get a furlough about July 1, Jeanie could think of little else.

"Of course we'll go up home," she told Pat at lunchtime.

Though no one could ever take Margie's place, she and Pat had become closer now that it was just the two of them eating lunch out on the fire escape.

89

"I don't want to make any plans until Kenny comes home, so I haven't written to his folks. It would be great to surprise them."

That same Monday evening, she was writing to Kenny when a knock startled her. A telegram! She held her breath as she opened it. WIRE MONEY FOR FURLOUGH IMMEDIATELY. LEAVING HERE WEDNESDAY NIGHT. LOVE KENNY.

It wasn't until the next day that she realized she'd forgotten to tip the Western Union boy. "I thought he was just hanging around long enough to know what was in the telegram," she told Pat. "I hope delivering good news was tip enough."

"When do you think Kenny will get here?" Pat asked.

"Saturday, I hope, but I really don't know. He can't phone me so I'll just have to wait. I never thought to give him Charles and Thelma's phone number."

"My husband's coming home on furlough," Jeanie told her boss. "I'll need to be off from work next week and maybe part of the following week, too."

Henry smiled and gave her a one-armed hug. "Come back as soon as you can."

How Jeanie wished she could share her good news with Margie. She didn't dare leave the house Saturday, so Friday night she shopped for food and then spent some time downstairs with Charles, Thelma, and baby Elizabeth. It felt so good to hold that tiny bundle. The baby had lots of dark hair and looked more like Charles than like Thelma, Jeanie thought. She was glad to know that Thelma's sister, Irene, had come to help her.

Jeanie purposely left some housecleaning for Saturday so she had something to do. She also shampooed and set her hair early in the morning and then put on some makeup.

Chapter Eight

Later she would change into that black skirt and red-and-white checked blouse that Kenny liked so much.

Several times she walked down to the el station and back because she was nervous and couldn't sit still.

At 3:00 she changed her clothes and combed her hair. At 3:30 she freshened her makeup and combed her hair again. She also again dusted the black tables. They were always dusty—especially when the windows were open. The train was less than half a block away, and each time it went by, coal soot blew in the windows. At 4:00 she swept the stairs and then sat down with the July issue of *Woman's Day*. She read a page and chuckled. She could not remember a thing she had read.

She didn't want to start cooking anything, because she had no idea when Kenny might come. She decided they would just have sandwiches.

At 5:00 she was eating a bologna sandwich when she looked up, and there he was at the screen door.

"Kenny!"

His muscles felt like rock, but his lips were tender as ever.

His eyes never left her as she set the table for their supper sandwiches. She could not believe how self-conscious and awkward she felt. What was he thinking? Did he notice that she was ten pounds heavier?

She felt better when they began to talk, trying to fill in all the blanks their letters couldn't.

Back in his arms again, she knew it was foolish to think he would be disappointed.

"Let's not see anyone until tomorrow," he whispered against her ear.

She nodded. Tonight belonged only to them.

Nine

In the morning when they were both trying to use the same mirror and he playfully flicked water over his shoulder at her, it seemed as if they had never been apart.

Jeanie knew he would soon be gone, and she wished they could spend every one of these precious hours by themselves. But she knew Vi was eager to see her soldier-brother.

When they arrived, Vi beamed as Kenny said, "Hey! You kids have sure grown since I've been gone." The children scrambled all over him. Art had a million questions about army life, but Vi just sat and listened. When they were ready to leave, Vi hugged Kenny and said, "When are you going up home? I know the folks are waiting to hear from you."

"We're going to take the train up Tuesday," Kenny said. "We'll call the folks from Merrill to come and pick us up."

Union Station was one flowing mass of uniforms and civilians. As Kenny and Jeanie parked their bags and waited for gate 15 to open, they heard a familiar voice yell, "Hey, Kenny!"

It was Spike, one of Kenny's best friends and high school classmates, whose parents now lived next door to Kenny's folks. There was back slapping and laughter, and Kenny said, "Man! I never thought we'd meet in Union Station."

The gate opened and the flood of traveling humanity streamed through. Jeanie picked up one of her bags and followed the two bantering guys.

A few yards into the station, she tripped, fell hard, and took the knee out of her precious nylon stocking. Before she could get up and grab her bag, the crowd had closed in between them and neither of the guys even knew she had fallen.

She boarded the train, but as always when she gave the conductor her destination, he told her, "Up ahead."

Her skinned knee stinging, she struggled through the heavy door to the next car as the train pulled out of the station. As it picked up speed and rounded corners she staggered from one side of the aisle to the other, and in each car the conductor said, "Up ahead."

Gradually people were seated, and by the time she got to the Merrill car, she was the only one struggling through the heavy door.

Kenny and Spike were standing in the aisle halfway down the car by the only empty seat. "Nice of them to save me a seat," she muttered to herself.

As she sat down, Kenny hoisted her bag up on the rack, kissed her quickly and said, "We're going to the club car for a smoke." He didn't even see her bleeding knee.

Left alone beside a dozing woman with bright red hair, Jeanie fumed. How inconsiderate could Kenny be? Anger, hurt, and disappointment churned within her. She had pictured hours and hours of togetherness on the train, and

CHAPTER NINE

here she was alone again, with a ruined nylon stocking and a bloody knee.

After a few moments, she went to the rest room to wash off the blood. The water made it hurt even more.

She hoped the guys would be back in a few minutes, and when those minutes grew to almost an hour, her thoughts went from, *He's inconsiderate. He doesn't even want to be with me. He doesn't love me.* At that point she realized her thinking had become ridiculous.

But how should she act? Hurt? Angry? Or should she play the martyr and act as if his leaving her meant nothing at all?

Before she could decide, the guys were back—still laughing and joking.

"Oh, my gosh! When did you do that?" Kenny asked. Her short skirt didn't begin to hide her oozing knee.

"I fell before we got on the train," she said evenly.

The lady seated next to her suddenly perked up. "I think I have a Band-Aid," she said, rummaging in her bag.

She did.

Kenny applied it. "Does it still hurt?"

Jeanie nodded, but smiled. He was back and that was all that mattered.

Kenny was careful to stay with her when they changed trains at New Lisbon. They even got seats together, and Spike sat on a suitcase in the aisle—like a lot of other people.

"Spike's folks are picking him up at Merrill," Kenny said, "so we won't even call my folks. We'll surprise 'em."

There were tears and greetings at Merrill when they met Spike's folks, and then it was an hour's ride to Rib Lake.

After they pulled up between the two houses, Spike and his parents went to Kenny's folks' back door instead of to

95

their own, and Kenny and Jeanie crouched down in the back of the car.

"Oh, Spike. You got a furlough!" they heard Kenny's mother exclaim when she opened the door. "I'm waiting to hear from Kenny. He's supposed to get one too."

She invited them in, and Kenny and Jeanie waited until they were all in the kitchen before they crept out and up to the door.

When Kenny's mother turned from filling the coffeepot, there they stood.

She set the pot down with a crash and screamed, "Kenny!" Then she laughed and cried and cried and laughed.

His dad stood in the doorway, brushing tears away with the back of his hand.

About an hour later, his mother, still shaking, shook her finger at Kenny. "Don't ever pull a surprise like that again. I thought I was going to have a heart attack."

The next two days were a whirlwind of visiting with relatives, running around town, and eating big meals. Friday, they drove out to the farm where Gram, teary-eyed, fiercely hugged them both. The next day she went along with them as they visited all around the country block.

Although it was fun to see everyone, Jeanie was happy when Sunday evening came and they boarded the train again for Chicago, tired and grateful to be alone again.

Only one more day. Monday they spent some time with Vi and Art and that evening walked up the street to the little ice-cream parlor for their favorite caramel sundaes topped with toasted, salted pecans.

"That's where Lu's parents live," Jeanie told him when they passed the street on their way home. "I may as well tell you . . . I don't like her. She's just not the kind of girl I want to be friends with. I just couldn't bring myself to write about it. I'm sorry 'cause I know you and Andy are good friends."

"I kinda wondered" Kenny said. "I kept finding out things about Lu that I knew you wouldn't like, but I didn't want to say anything until you did."

Jeanie groaned. "And I thought I had to be friends with her because you guys were such good friends."

Kenny spun her around. "Listen! You use your own judgment. Don't let me or anyone else tell you who you should or shouldn't be friends with."

Back home, they asked Thelma to snap some pictures of them sitting together on the warm grass in the backyard. Jeanie thought the lump in her throat would surely show on the pictures.

Tuesday came much too soon, and Jeanie's knees felt weak as she watched Kenny pack. Again, her future was just a dark tunnel.

At 3:00 he said, "It's time." Wordlessly, they held each other close. Everything had already been said.

He didn't say good-bye, but at the door he turned, winked and said, "See you next trip around."

As before, he didn't look back as he crossed the street, and again she waited until the el train rumbled away before letting the sobs come.

It was as if she was back in that dark night again. There was nothing ahead but overseas duty, and only God knew how long it would be before she saw him again.

That night she wrote a long, loving letter to Kenny, so it would be waiting for him when he got back to camp.

She was glad she had to pack her lunch and get ready for work the next day. Often Gram said that work was a blessing, but Jeanie had never understood what the older woman had meant—until now.

97

"Oh, how can anything hurt so bad," she groaned when she went to bed. She told herself that thousands of other couples were hurting too, but that really didn't help.

She knew from experience that once the he-was-just-here-a-little-while-ago feeling faded, she would hurt less. That helped.

Still it was like trying to live with a toothache, because the hurting inside never left. She had learned, too, that striving to relive those tender moments only made her more lonesome.

At work the next day, Jeanie knew she had to get back to the one thing that had helped her in the past—the resolve to make good use of her time. She vaguely remembered being enthusiastic a few weeks ago. It would be wonderful to feel like that again.

Halfheartedly, she began a list of things she could do. One of them was contacting her friend Gen, who always inspired her. Gen could sew circles around her; knew how to get around in the city; knew what was in good taste; and she was caring, always smiling, and fun to be with. Jeanie wondered why she hadn't called her long ago.

Another thing she would do was help Vi as often as she could without becoming a pest. There was always a basket of sprinkled clothes to iron, dishes to be washed, little ones to bathe and change. If nothing else, she could always work the little yellow capsule of color into the margarine.

That evening she knew the darkness in her world was beginning to lift.

Her first word from Kenny was a postcard mailed from Omaha while he was still on the train. He said it was a nicer train than the one he'd come home on, but there were no

CHAPTER NINE

seats, so he had to sleep in the little room next to the restroom. It took four days to get from Chicago to Oregon.

The next day, July 20, British and American paratroopers landed in Sicily.

"Just think," Pat said at noon, "they could have used our cords on their parachutes."

Jeanie couldn't work hard enough that day and smiled with satisfaction at the stack of spool trays at the end of her machines that evening.

The next day headlines announced that US planes had bombed Rome.

A few days later, Mussolini resigned, and the US Seventh Army took Palermo, Sicily. Meanwhile Jeanie read that the Soviet offensive had spread across the entire eastern front. Things were beginning to happen.

If only there was more she could do to help end this war. She rarely bought a newspaper so she didn't have many papers to save. She always cut the ends out of soup and vegetable cans, tucked them inside and flattened them with her foot. She saved every drop of grease from her little bit of cooking, but she had yet to fill a one-pound Crisco can. There must be something more she could do.

She had money taken out of her paycheck each week for war bonds, but she couldn't take out any more and expect to pay her rent and carfare and buy food and an occasional piece of material to sew a new skirt, blouse, or dress. Except for the money she had sent Kenny for his trip home and for the watch she had bought for him, her army wife's allotment check went right into the bank.

Jeanie didn't realize how much that watch meant to Kenny until she got the letter he wrote when he got back to Pendleton. He said it was something he would never part

99

with, because she gave it to him, and it would always remind him of those wonderful furlough days. "If every couple loved each other as much as we do," he wrote, "wouldn't it be a wonderful world?"

In his next letter, his world was anything but wonderful. They had returned from an all-day convoy at 5:30, and right after chow they were called to classes until 8:30. Then he and a friend named Miller and some other guys went to the PX. When someone came to tell them they were wanted at the barracks, they stalled until a sergeant came and told them to go. When they still didn't go, a first lieutenant came.

"Boy, were we in trouble! When we got back we found out all they wanted us for was scrubbing the barracks. We knew most of the guys had gone to the movies, so we had to do it alone. This place is going nuts. Today we saw the CO about the trouble we were in, and he restricted us to camp for the weekend. I can't wait to get out of here."

Jeanie prayed he wouldn't get into more trouble.

She breathed a sigh of relief when he wrote in his next letter that he had gone to church. He admitted he had been a bad boy, "an' dat ain't good, is it?"

When he wrote later that he had gotten two shots for yellow fever and typhus, she was sure he was headed for the South Pacific.

All she knew about the war in the Pacific was that there was a lot of "island hopping," trying to establish US air bases.

Kenny's letter of August 6 started Jeanie dreaming about their future. He wrote, "Darling, I figure we'd better take our trip out West before we have any children, so you and I can be alone together. When I get out of this army, I want to be with you all alone so we can catch up on our loving."

CHAPTER NINE

All the next day at work she fantasized about their trip. Would they camp? Stay in tourist cabins or lodges? She dreamed of long hikes to beautiful lakes—maybe even a skinny-dip if it wasn't too cold. And there would be waterfalls and snowcapped mountains and clear mountain streams. At night they'd sit by a fire and marvel at the stars. . . .

In Sunday night's letter to Kenny she wrote,

> I went to see Gen this afternoon. She lives right off North Avenue near Austin, so I only had to take one streetcar. She's trying to fill the time the way I am but is doing a better job and had given me all sorts of good ideas. You should see what she has sewn—tailored. She lent me a couple patterns, and I know I'm going to learn a lot just from following the instructions. "She's as pretty as ever— *beautiful* is a better word. You remember those big, deep-set blue eyes and her beautiful smile. The best part is that she's so nice. Can't you just hear her laugh? Every Monday night, she goes to Judson Baptist Church to work on Red Cross bandages. She invited me to come for dinner, stay overnight, and roll bandages with her and a girlfriend, Ellie. I'm so excited! I've been wanting to do something more for the war effort but just didn't know where or how. Isn't it great of her to want me to stay over and everything?

The next evening, sitting on the top bunk in Gen's room, Jeanie wrote,

> It has been a special evening. Gen's folks are so nice to me. But I'm a little disappointed with the bandage work. I don't think we accomplished very much. We were folding four-inch squares and had to use a ruler to measure them just so. The gauze wasn't cut on the grain, and it

101

was really hard to fold it. Oh well, I guess it adds up if enough women do it.

Kenny warned her that he had a thousand-mile convoy coming up, so she wasn't too concerned when she didn't get any letters for a few days.

Then on August 18, she got a postcard from Boise, Idaho, telling her they were headed for Washington. He was sad because he had broken the crystal on his new watch.

When he wrote again, he said they were back in Pendleton. It had been a tough trip, sleeping on the ground, but the scenery was beautiful. That scenery must have put him in a romantic mood, because he wrote one of the most loving letters Jeanie had ever received, reminiscing about their wedding. "It was the happiest day of my life, the day we got married, but I didn't think you'd ever stop shaking."

Jeanie spent much of the following day thinking about their wedding of almost a year ago. Most of her plans had not worked out, and she had been a nervous wreck by the time she walked up the aisle. Try as she might, she could not stop shaking, and the fern in her bouquet had telegraphed every tremble to the whole congregation—and to Kenny.

"Say hello to your friend Gen," he wrote in his next letter. "She's a swell girl. I felt good after you wrote that you had been there. That's the most excited you've been for a long time."

On September 3, Jeanie heard on the radio that the British Eighth Army had landed on the Italian coast. Then five days later, the Italian armistice was announced, and shortly afterward the naval fleet and air force surrendered to the Allies.

But that good news was quickly followed by bad news. The Germans had launched a counterattack near Salerno,

CHAPTER NINE

and the Allied beachhead was seriously threatened. There were several tense days until the Germans withdrew on September 17.

Meanwhile, Kenny was getting a variety of training. "We blew up a barn with a booby trap today," he wrote, "and then had to fight the fire until we got it out. I smell like a smokehouse."

Jeanie chuckled. She could almost smell the old smokehouse where Gram smoked hams and bacon in the fall, and fish in the spring.

He wrote on September 21,

> I just got done working. It's 10:30 and the lights are out, so I'm writing this in the latrine. There are rumors flying all over the place. We could be really shipping out. We're restricted to base and can't even go to the PX without signing out.

Jeanie had a rough day, trying to get used to the idea of Kenny being someplace overseas.

"I read in the *Rib Lake Herald* that Spike is in North Africa," he wrote September 22. "Sure wonder where I'm going. I can't tell you all I know, but I'll tell you all I can, whenever I can."

The next day he sent her his APO address—New York City. Jeanie was relieved. At least he wasn't going to the South Pacific.

Jeanie's heart did a flip-flop when she opened the next letter. In it were papers for her to sign giving her power of attorney. "If I should be missing in action, they'd send you a check after twelve months for any money I had coming, but it would be in my name and you'd have to sign it,"

103

Kenny wrote. "But don't worry, darling 'cause I'm coming back to you—and in one piece!"

The letter had no postmark, and there were little sections cut out of it—her first censored letter.

For the first time in weeks Jeanie cried herself to sleep.

Ever since Emma had heard that Kenny might soon be going overseas, the young couple had been heavy on her heart. Today, September 26, their first anniversary; she ached for them.

It was pleasant out on the porch swing, with just a gentle, autumn breeze—enough to make a sweater feel good. Last year they had woken to snow-laden trees, and when it was time for the ceremony, the ground had been covered with slush.

Emma studied the garden. The weary, old tomato plants and cornstalks needed to be pulled out. She'd get it done a little at a time.

Her thoughts went back to Jeanie's wedding. Such a pathetic little wedding. No frills. But then Emma thought, *It's just like I told her last year when she was so upset by the snow: The wedding is only for a day; the marriage is for a lifetime.* She smiled now, thinking of those loving glances between them last summer when Kenny was on furlough. In spite of being apart so much, it appeared their marriage was alive and well.

But now he probably was on his way overseas. Emma sighed. How long would this old war last? There didn't seem to be any turnaround, except down in Italy. All those boys!

Chapter Nine

There was so little she could do—stretch her quarter of a pound of butter to last the week, savor that one cup of coffee a day, and knit socks for her grandsons in service. So little. So little. Ah, but she could pray—and there was more power in prayer than in all the war bonds and war plants combined. Every time she felt useless, she would remind herself to pray for all the boys in service, for all their leaders, and for those waiting at home.

Kenny's September 30 letter again bore no postmark. "I've got a few minutes to write now, but I don't know what to write." In his next nonpostmarked letter he wrote, "I know what I want to write, but I can't write it. I can tell you that I made out a class-E allotment today, so you should get another twenty dollars a month."

She pictured him on a train headed East and found out she was right when October 3 he wrote that he was still in the "good old US of A," on the East coast. "Ray will soon be graduating from OCS training. Congratulate him for me, and tell him I'll write as soon as I can—when I find out where he is."

Then day after day passed with no letters.

Jeanie spent more time at Vi's and downstairs with Thelma and the baby and Monday nights with Gen. But her heart was with Kenny—wherever he was.

Another whole week. Still no letter. No special war progress news either.

On October 16 there was a big splash in the papers about the opening of Chicago's first subway. Jeanie was only mildly

105

interested. Someday, she promised herself, she'd take a ride on it, but right now she had more important things to do.

Jeanie found some comfort rereading Kenny's recent letters, but she avoided the one about giving her power of attorney.

It seemed there would never be another letter. It wasn't easy to be cheerful when people asked about Kenny. She felt like the invisible bond between them was no longer taut, but tangled. One night she dreamed she was searching and searching, but couldn't find him. He was somewhere out there, but where was somewhere?

When she saw white in the mailbox she no longer got excited. Most of the time it was only an advertisement or a letter from someone else. But October 29 there was an odd little envelope—a V-mail.

It was a tiny photocopied letter in Kenny's dear handwriting with "England" at the top. It was, of course, brief. "Just a word to let you know I'm safe and feeling swell. Can't say anymore than that, so I'll close. Write lots. Don't be afraid of what you write. Your letters aren't censored. Only mine are."

England!

She didn't know if that was good or bad, but at least she knew where he was. She ran downstairs to show the V-mail letter to Thelma.

Ten

"I'm still drifting along on a pleasant cloud of memory this evening," Jeanie wrote to Kenny early in October. "I started thinking about when you were home this summer, the day we broke away from everyone to take a walk down by the river. This afternoon I hardly knew I was working, because I could feel the breeze across the pasture and hear the killdeer and the lazy, old river. The songs from *Oklahoma* kept going through my mind that day, and I was singing snatches now and then as we walked up the slope to where the old log house used to stand. I told you how much I loved the rhythm and the lyrics of The Surrey with the Fringe on Top, and you said, 'You always just love something,' and I turned into your arms and said, 'Especially you!' And we stood there unaware of anything but each other. You smelled like fresh air and sunshine. We'd probably be there yet if the mosquitoes hadn't found us.

"As we walked on past the little stillborn baby's grave, I told you about Aunt Ella and how she thought it was all her fault the baby was born dead, because she was so angry that her mother was having another baby.

"I pointed out the stones and high grass that had once been the foundation of Gram and Grandpa's little log house. We tried to imagine how it had looked and where the barn must have stood. I said I couldn't, for the life of me, imagine my big uncles Al and Fred and George and the rest or Aunt Ella and my other aunts ever being chubby, little, barefoot children, and you said, 'Or your grandma young and slim.'

"We crawled under the barbed-wire fence and sat with our backs against a big elm tree. You laughed when I said we were probably sitting right where the old outhouse had stood. Gram used to point to that tree and say, 'That tree was only as tall as the outhouse when we moved to the big house.'

"We looked over at the white house across the swamp and the big, old red barn—badly in need of paint—and you said you bet they hated to leave this spot.

"I agreed, and said probably the only thing the same about this spot now was the sound of the river—and maybe even that had changed because the water is so much lower than back in those days.

"Oh, the war seemed so far away that day, and for a little while, we were able to forget we had another parting ahead of us.

"When you first left last January, I drove myself half crazy trying to feel how it was when we were together. But no matter how hard I tried, I couldn't feel it again. Today I discovered that memories can be comforting if I don't try too hard to feel those thrills and simply let the happy memories flow. Songs help too, don't they? All the way home on the streetcar, I had Oh, What a Beautiful Morning going through my head, and I was relaxed—almost happy. I wonder if maybe

God inspired the writing of *Oklahoma,* because He knew we'd need some light-hearted music this year.

"Tonight, it doesn't hurt quite so much that you're way over there in England, because it's like I've been with you all afternoon."

How Jeanie wished she could see Kenny's face as he read that letter.

Kenny's letter of October 25 was signed "corporal," but he didn't mention getting his new rank. Surely he would have said something about getting it. That letter was probably still on the way. This one was written in light pencil, on both sides of the paper, with sections cut out here and there. It was quite a challenge for Jeanie to read. She imagined it was an even greater challenge for the company commander, who had to censor all those letters.

In his next letter, Kenny wrote that he was in a nice camp with four men to a room and that the grub was good. He also told her,

> When we moved from Oregon to the East Coast, we went right through ——— [the word was cut out] and right past ——— Rubber Company where I worked, and we sat in the ——— station for over and hour. I couldn't get off the train. If I ever was tempted to go AWOL, it was then. I felt sick all over until the next day. I still get mad when I think about it, but I have to let it go.

Jeanie let out a cry. Oh, if only she had known—she might have talked to him through the train window, or something. But Kenny was right. They had to let it go.

That night her letter included two requests: that he write on only one side of the paper and that he use a pen for V-Mail. Pencil was nearly impossible to read.

109

Jeanie wrote him the big news November 15. "You have a new little nephew! Robert—Bobby. (Now they have Buddy, Billy, and Bobby!) Art says he has a lot of hair. I can't wait to see him, and I'm so glad he's here. Vi's fine now, but she had a long labor. Last week she looked as if she could hardly go another step."

Day after day, Kenny wrote, "No mail," and each letter was shorter and sadder. Finally, November 30 he wrote,

> This is one happy day! I got twenty-nine letters—twenty-three of them from you. I put them in order by date and I'm reading them whenever I get time. I feel like a different guy. I saw your cousin Earl's name on a Red Cross roster yesterday, so I know he's around here somewhere. There are probably a lot of guys I know near me, but there's no way to track them down.

Jeanie hugged his V-mail letter written December 3, that said each night he was reading one of the devotionals in the book they used during those months before he went into service. With his next letter, which was not a V-mail, he sent a copy of "Lover's Prayer," which someone had given him.

> Heavenly Father up above
> Please protect the woman I love
> Keep her always safe and sound
> No matter when or where she's bound
> Help her to know and help her to see
> And then, dear Lord, help me to be
> The kind of man she wants me to be
> Help me always please to do
> The kind of things that will prove me true.
> Keep us now, keep us forever
> Happy, loving and always together.

CHAPTER TEN

Kenny said he had no idea who had written the poem.

Again his mail was held up, and it hurt Jeanie to get letters day after day saying, "No mail."

Where, she wondered, was the carefully packed Christmas box she had sent?

Christmas was on Saturday, and Jeanie thought she would beat the crowd by taking the train to Wisconsin Thursday evening. She was in for a big surprise. Ticket agents seemed not to care that there were more people than seats, and when everyone shoved their way aboard the train, the first ones on got seats. Jeanie found a seat in the little lounge section by the rest room, but it was so packed with luggage she barely had room for her feet.

After changing trains at New Lisbon, she got a regular seat, and though she slept a bit, she was exhausted when she got off the train at Tomahawk. But as soon as she saw Roy and Gram waiting for her at the station, she forgot how tired she was. Why was it that Gram seemed smaller every time she saw her?

On the drive home Gram talked mostly about how the war was affecting each family. "Ella's worried about Myrtle's husband being drafted. He works in a shipyard down on the Illinois River, you know." She shook her head. "I always forget the name of the place. Well, he's been deferred twice already, but the next time he may have to go."

"But Myrtle's having another baby!" Jeanie protested. "Surely they wouldn't draft a father of three."

111

Gram sighed and her brow furrowed. "I know, but I read way back in October that fathers will be drafted now."

It was good to see her cousins Grace and Ruby and all her other relatives at the Christmas Eve service. Grace's husband Ralph would probably go overseas soon. Chet had been gone almost two years, Ruby said.

There was no tinsel in the stores this year, so all Jeanie had for decorating Gram's Christmas tree were a few limp strands saved from last year.

While Gram rocked and knitted, Jeanie trimmed the little tree as she had for so many years. Christmas carols and war news from Roy and Helen's radio broke the silence.

Her throat ached when she remembered last Christmas Eve when she and Kenny had trimmed Gram's tree together. Surely by next Christmas, Kenny would be home, and they'd be here together again.

It was as if Gram read her thoughts. "Oh, a year goes fast," she said with a wave of her hand. "By next year all the boys will be home for Christmas."

Jeanie wanted to tell her that when you are seventy-four, a year probably does go fast, but when you are only nineteen, a year seems like ages.

Gram went to bed, and then there was nothing for Jeanie to do but to curl up in her cold, empty bed and, aching with loneliness, pray that the war would end soon.

Later that week, Kenny's parents came to take her for an evening at their home. It was good to see them. She learned that Ray was still in the States but would probably be going overseas soon. "I told him, 'For goodness sake, be good to your men,'" his mother said. "I've heard that if the men don't like an officer, they won't give a darn if he's in danger—might even shoot him themselves!"

CHAPTER TEN

Jeanie assured her Ray would be good to his men. They smiled when she told them how Ray used to tease her when they marched side by side in the high school band. "He'd get out of step, yell at me to get in step with him, take a skip, and get back in step. And then he would laugh when Mr. Spiedel yelled at me for being out of step."

It was good to see them at least smile. There wasn't much to smile about these days.

Eleven

Back in her little apartment, Jeanie struggled to regain her emotional balance. Even though it had been good to be in Wisconsin, coming back to her lonely life was all the more painful.

The one bright star in the black night of her life these days was Kenny's letters.

When he answered her letter telling him about little Bobby's birth, he said, "Won't it be swell when we have our own children? I can just see our little Kent and Joannie. I wonder if we will have just those two. Maybe we'll end up with a dozen or so."

Jeanie loved it when he wrote about their children. How many guys his age, she wondered, thought that much about having children?

In his next letter, he sent another poem written by some guy in his company:

As I lay down to sleep last night,
I heard my dog tag say,

> "Don't worry I'm your friend, my lad,
> I'm with you night and day.
> And if death should ever part us,
> Don't let it make you blue.
> For I'll prove that I am faithful
> By going home for you."
> Now it's true my dog tag's faithful
> And goes where 'ere I roam.
> But I sure will do my d——
> To beat my dog tags home.

"I'll beat mine home by a long shot," he assured her, "because I know what I'm going home to, and my dog tags don't."

In the middle of January, Jeanie finally learned that Kenny had received her Christmas box and two other packages on Christmas Eve. In hers she had packed a pair of woolen socks Gram knitted for him, and he said he was touched to think of all those hours she'd spent knitting and, no doubt, praying for him.

"When I saw that package with my initials in red tape on the corner, the first thing I thought of was last Christmas when we wrapped packages on our front-room floor."

Jeanie remembered last Christmas too. Colored Scotch tape had been new, and they had had a lot of fun decorating packages with initials and streamline designs—until she criticized the way he was doing it.

He tossed the tape at her and growled, "Here! You do it if you're so fussy."

The spirit of the evening abruptly changed from light-hearted intimacy to peevish anger.

He acts like a little boy, she had thought. *I can't say one thing and he gets mad. Well, he can just get over it. I'm not going to apologize.*

116

CHAPTER ELEVEN

Tearfully, she wrapped the rest of the packages while he sat and smoked. After she'd finished and had packed them to take home, he tried to hug her, but she brushed him away. Their precious evening was ruined, and hugs wouldn't fix it. When it was time to read from the devotional book and to pray together, Jeanie knew she couldn't go to sleep without their little nightly ritual. She crept up to him and said, "I'm sorry. I shouldn't criticize you."

He groaned and hugged her tight. "I don't know why I get so mad when you tell me I'm not doing something right." He kissed her and kissed her.

Jeanie sighed and tucked the letter away. She knew then that she had much to learn about this husband of hers, but when he got home after all his army experiences, she would probably have a great deal more to learn.

He wrote another letter on Christmas Eve just before midnight.

> I was going to write that I wish you were here, but I don't. I wouldn't wish this place on anyone—especially you. I wish I was with you! I can just see you trimming Gram's tree and putting the presents under it like we did last year. I can't feel any Christmas spirit here. There's no Christmas music—nothing. We did get some Cokes, and a couple of us got together. We ate cookies and drank Cokes and talked awhile.
> Your lonesome soldier.

New Year's Day he wrote that he was in bed at midnight because they were restricted to base and there was nothing else to do. He said he got her December 8 letter and wondered where it had it been all that while.

The next paragraph made her gasp.

It seems like everyone in the States thinks this war is just about over. As far as I can see, it's just starting for us. But I always pray that it will end sooner than we think, because I just don't think I can stand to be away from you another year.

Just starting for us.
That night Jeanie felt that awful darkness again.

In January, the Allies landed on the Italian mainland at Anzio, and Jeanie began buying a newspaper every night. She needed to see the maps and arrows to understand what the radio newscasters were saying. Surrounded by the Germans, the US troops were fighting desperately to hold their beachhead, while other Allied troops were attempting to break through near Cassino.

Was Chet, her cousin Ruby's boyfriend, among those troops? she wondered. How many other men she knew were fighting there?

The war in the Pacific was still a puzzle to her. She knew US troops landed on the Marshall Islands, but she wasn't sure how important that victory was to winning the war.

"Did you see the new lady?" Pat asked Jeanie when she stopped by her machines one morning in February. "Her name is Kate."

Jeanie nodded. "I saw her, but I didn't get to talk with her. How old do you think she is?"

Chapter Eleven

Pat shrugged. "Close to forty maybe?"

"She looks friendly. Why don't we ask her to eat with us."

"Fine with me. Oh-oh, here comes the boss," said Pat.

Kate was delighted when they asked her to join them for lunch, and she flashed a smile that showed the glint of a gold molar on her left side. Unusually tall, she wore her long, blond hair wound up in a swirl on the top of her head—a becoming style on her.

That noon Pat and Jeanie learned that Kate's son, Larry, who was not much younger than they were, had just gone into the army.

Jeanie felt a pang of sympathy for Kate, though she couldn't see how it could hurt as much as parting with a husband. She knew Kate was having a hard time because she couldn't talk about Larry without getting teary-eyed. "He's in infantry boot camp now in Tennessee, but who knows where he'll be sent from there."

More and more Jeanie was grateful that Kenny was behind the steering wheel of a truck in the Quartermaster Corps.

That Sunday, the pastor's sermon was all about worry. Usually his sermons were merely a stream of words flowing past Jeanie's ears, but today, she caught hold of them. "Worry," he said, "is a sin, because one cannot trust God and worry at the same time."

Jeanie had never thought of worry as being sin.

He quoted a number of scriptures, and Jeanie remembered the one in Philippians, chapter 4, about not being full of care about anything, but rather, praying about it and getting one's mind on good things. That made sense. It seemed Gram said something like that a long time ago. She wished

119

she had listened more, instead of having turned her thoughts to other things when Gram had had something to say.

The next few days, Jeanie kept thinking about that sermon and even wrote Kenny about it. She wished she could talk about it with Kate, but she didn't know where to start. All she knew about Kate's faith was that she went to Mass every morning, and Mass was a mystery to Jeanie.

In March, headlines announced the first daylight, US Air Force air raid on Berlin. Jeanie shuddered to think of what the people must be going through. What a terrible price to pay. If only it would help end the war.

Then the daffodils bloomed again. Surely, before they bloomed once more, Kenny would be home. But, however long it took, she knew it was her duty to spend that time wisely.

Weeks marched by in an orderly progression: church and then to Vi's on Sunday; bandage work and overnight with Gen on Monday; laundry on Tuesday; sewing or some other household chore on Wednesday; to Vi's on Thursday; and babysitting with Elizabeth on Friday.

Charles was working two jobs now, so Thelma needed someone to stay with Elizabeth when she directed the church choir Friday evenings. "I can write letters as easily down here as upstairs," Jeanie had told her, and it gave Jeanie a sense of satisfaction to know she was doing two important things at one time.

Jeanie would gladly work every Saturday. But every now and then, for reasons she didn't understand, they would not have to work, and though she liked earning all that

Chapter Eleven

overtime pay, it was nice to sleep as long as she wanted those Saturday mornings.

Helen wrote, "It looks like we'll be able to get Gram moved into her own little house this spring. We hope you can come home at Easter time and help get her settled."

"I wonder how Gram will like having a little house of her own after living so close to everyone in the big house all those years?" Jeanie told Thelma one evening in March. "Roy and Helen's family need more room, so Roy bought a little three-room house and had it moved just west of the big house."

"Has your grandmother written anything about it?" Thelma asked.

"Only that the house was moved now and Roy was digging a deep trench for the waterline. It has to be deep up there," Jeanie explained, "or the water will freeze in winter."

When Jeanie went up home at the end of March, she found Gram trying to be enthusiastic about the new house. "The windows are almost the same in the living room and bedroom, but now I'll have a nice south window in the kitchen. That will be so nice in winter, and I'll be able to look way across the field to where the old log house stood." Leave it to Gram to find something positive about it. Still, Jeanie was sure she hated to leave Roy's big house.

The week went fast as Jeanie helped with some painting and moving small items into the little house, but it still wasn't finished when she had to go back to Chicago, and the real moving day would come a bit later.

She wrote to Kenny, "It will seem so odd to have Gram living in that little house, instead of those rooms we lived in. I feel like my home, as I knew it, will be gone. But then, that's the way life is—change, change, change."

121

Twelve

The last week in April, Jeanie got a note from her cousin Myrtle. They had a new little Bobby—just like Vi had—born April 22. "Would you be able to come down and be his godmother on May 14?" Myrtle wrote. "We've asked Harold to be his godfather. I hope it can be that weekend, because Harry will be moving us up to Mom and Dad's the last week in May. He got his 'greetings' the day we brought Bobby home."

Jeanie dashed downstairs to tell Thelma the good and the bad news. "Myrtle's such a special, capable person, but it's going to be so hard for her with those three little ones. Hazy's just three, and little Harry was just a year in February and Bobby so tiny."

Later Jeanie wondered how Thelma felt, knowing that Charles would never be drafted because of his bad leg. Thankful, she was sure, but maybe a little guilty, too, that they couldn't do their part to help end the war. Anyone who didn't do everything they possibly could for the war effort was frowned upon these days. The next day, Jeanie explained to her boss that she needed to be off that Saturday. He grinned. "Oh, I don't think it would delay the progress of the war too much if you took off."

After Jeanie had checked the train schedule, she wrote to Myrtle and told her she would be there for baby Bobby's baptism.

Harry met her at the train, eyes sparkling and smiling as always. "I think it'll be good for Myrt to see how well you've managed since Kenny's gone," he said, opening the car door for her. "You know, the folks up home think you're doing really great."

Jeanie felt her face flush. "Yes, but I don't have three little ones . . ." The lump in her throat kept her from finishing.

"Well, at least I'm young and healthy," Harry said. "It's better for me to go than the guys in their late thirties. Can you imagine some of those office workers going through boot camp?"

Oh, it was good to see Myrtle. Her cheeks were as rosy as ever, but she had deep, dark circles under her eyes.

Little Hazy was as cute as a little girl could be, with eyes like violets and dimples that appeared in unexpected places when she talked or smiled. Little Harry clung to his playpen rail and studied Jeanie with huge blue eyes.

"Oh, he's adorable!" Jeanie exclaimed.

"Come see!" Myrtle said, leading the way to the one bedroom.

"Oh, he's so little." Jeanie whispered. Baby Bobby looked lost, lying on his tummy with his little knees drawn under him in the middle of a crib.

When they were back in the other room—a combined living room and kitchen—Myrtle said, "At least I won't miss this place."

CHAPTER TWELVE

Jeanie could see why. The shipyard workers lived in long, barrack-like buildings. Though each unit had a front and back door and a front and back window, only the end units had windows on the side. It was like living in a cavern, Jeanie thought.

"The porch is the worst part," Myrtle said as they stood by the front door, looking out on the rutted ground between the rows of buildings. A wooden porch ran the full length of the building, giving children a great place to ride their squeaky tricycles or run from one end to the other. "And talk about living in a fishbowl. A person has to leave the curtains open for air and for light, and everyone walking by can look right in."

The next morning, Jeanie got to see the backyard. As far as she could see, diapers and other laundry fluttered from sagging lines.

"You can see this was a cornfield a couple years ago," Myrtle said. There were still dead cornstalks along the deep drainage ditch. "I can't let Hazy out of my sight for a minute because of that old ditch. We started complaining as soon as we moved in, and they promised to put up a fence, but that was almost two years ago. I just hope some child doesn't have to drown to get their attention." She shook her head. "I'm ashamed of myself complaining about things like this. What if we had to run off to bomb shelters?"

Sunday in church, Jeanie's knees felt shaky when Myrtle put little Bobby in her arms and she, Harold, and the baby went up to the baptismal font. The pastor had just began the sacrament when Hazy charged up to the font, yanked on the pastor's robe, and yelled, "What are you doing to my baby!"

Quickly, her uncle Harold scooped her up so she could see what was going on, and the ceremony proceeded.

125

As Long as I Have You

That afternoon Grace and Harold and their year-old Chuckie joined them for a picnic in a small park area in Seneca. "It's not much of a park," Myrtle said, "but it's better than trying to visit back home."

No one talked about Harry going into service, but Jeanie watched Grace swinging on a park swing, her red hair gleaming in the sunshine, and Chuckie sitting on her lap, and Jeanie wondered what Grace was thinking. Unless there were some spectacular victories, Harold, too, would have to leave Grace and little Chuckie.

Riding back on the train that evening, Jeanie felt a jumble of emotions. It had been wonderful to be in the midst of laughter and lighthearted banter, but each time she saw Harry playing with one of the children or holding tiny Bobby, her heart felt as if it was being squeezed.

Yet in a way, she almost envied Myrtle. At least she would still have her babies to love and to cuddle. Unless Jeanie held Elizabeth or Vi's little ones, there were days and days that she didn't touch another human being. She wondered if that was why she was feeling so strange lately, as if she wasn't part of the life around her but was merely observing it through a window.

Of course she had a lot to write to Kenny. "I can see why Myrtle's not sad to leave that place. Those walls are so thin you can hear everything next door. During the night, a baby cried and cried, but its parents just kept snoring away. In the morning, I asked Myrtle if she'd heard it, and she groaned and rolled her eyes. 'I've learned to tune it out, because I can't do a thing about it. I try to remember how fortunate we are that we're not being bombed.'"

A few days later the Allied forces captured Cassino, in Italy, which meant that now an all-out offensive could be

CHAPTER TWELVE

launched against the Germans. Then, on June 4, the Allies entered Rome. Jeanie rejoiced at all the progress.

June 6, 1944, began like any other Tuesday morning. At her machines, Jeanie's mind was on her recent trip to Seneca, and she wondered if Myrtle was settled in Wisconsin. Then, about three in the afternoon a mechanic ran from worker to worker shouting, "The Allies invaded the French coast!"

Word got around that the churches were open for prayer, so after work, Jeanie walked the few blocks to church, her thoughts swirling with a million questions and as many fears. "Where is Kenny?"

In church, people were scattered here and there, praying quietly. Words, which usually came easily to Jeanie, were strangely missing when she tried to pray. Everything she thought of praying, *Keep our boys safe* or *Help them win,* seemed so inadequate. And what about all those German soldiers? Tears ran unheeded as she simply whispered, "Jesus! Jesus!"

After what seemed like a long while, the blond girl beside her smiled at her through her tears and got up to leave. Jeanie decided it was time for her to leave too.

At the door the girl, who seemed to be about Jeanie's age, turned and asked, "Do you have a brother over there?"

Jeanie shook her head and choked, "Husband."

As they walked together down the stairs, the girl told Jeanie her name was Lenore and that she lived a few blocks up the street. "I remember seeing you, but I just never talked to you."

Jeanie said that, though she had gone to the church for over two years, no one but the pastor ever spoke to her. "People just nod and smile, but they don't say anything."

127

"Oh, I'm so sorry." Lenore said. She added that she had grown up in that church and knew many people. "We have a young people's group, and you'd be more than welcome to come. Of course it's all girls now."

Riding home on the streetcar, Jeanie had the feeling she had found a new friend.

At the corner newsstand, people were snatching papers, and Jeanie saw the big bold headline: D-DAY! ALLIES INVADE NORMANDY COAST. Jeanie didn't wait in line to buy a paper. Instead, hoping to hear more recent news on the radio, she hurried home.

An excited voice replaced the usual newscaster, and Jeanie strained to hear his words through the crackle of shortwave static. It was some time before she figured out that "Omaha" and "Utah" were stretches of beach where US troops had landed.

The rest of the world seemed to be standing still as Jeanie strained to hear what had happened. One thing she heard loud and clear. There were heavy casualties on Omaha beach, somewhat lighter casualties on Utah.

Her body grew more rigid by the minute as one question pounded over and over in her mind: *Where is Kenny?*

As the broadcast continued, she could picture the landing craft, the dead soldiers on the beaches, the gunfire from the ships offshore. She thought of the battles she had seen in newsreels, the men franticly running from one foxhole to another. . . .

Had Kenny been on one of those landing craft? Was he on shore or about to drive his truck down into the water?

Jesus! Jesus! she cried inwardly.

Over and over she repeated Philippians 4:6. "Don't be careful, meaning "anxious," about anything . . ."

CHAPTER TWELVE

She cowered beside the radio until dusk and then went down to talk with Thelma. She hadn't even thought about eating.

"Charles thinks Kenny is probably still in England," said Thelma. The quartermaster corps will be needed to keep hauling supplies to the English coast as the invasion moves on."

Jeanie blinked back tears.

Thelma's assurance provided a tiny fragment of hope to ease her anxious heart through the long, night hours.

Thirteen

The morning after D-Day, Jeanie saw smiles on the usually somber faces of fellow travelers on the streetcar. Some people were even talking to each other.

One old man slapped another one on the back. "Now we're getting somewhere!"

"Yes," the other agreed, "Ain't gonna be easy, but we've got a toehold."

That evening Jeanie forgot about things she had planned to do. Her heart thumped as she sat cross-legged on the floor, listening intently to one news broadcast after another. At one point, an on-the-spot reporter on Utah beach described vehicles coming up from the water and read the names printed on them—"Sweetheart Mary Beth," "Lu Lu, My Love," "Kissin' Katie," and others.

Jeanie held her breath. Kenny had sent a picture of his truck with "My Baby Jeanie" painted across the hood. If she heard that name, she didn't know how she could stand it, because it would mean Kenny was in the thick of the fighting.

She didn't hear that name, but she scarcely breathed until the newscast was over.

Later she almost wished she had heard it. At least she would know that he had made it to shore. But *Jeanie* was a fairly common name, so she still couldn't have been positive it was Kenny's truck.

At Utah beach, the invading troops were definitely making headway, but she heard that at Omaha beach the fighting was fierce. However, a beachhead had definitely been established. All the while she listened she wanted to scream, "Where is Kenny?"

In his letter, written May 26, which arrived the day after D-Day, he didn't even hint at the coming invasion. But Jeanie was sure he must have been hauling material to English ports and knew it was being planned. He wrote, "Darling, I don't know what I'd do if I didn't have you and our happy future ahead of us. I guess I'd just go bugs running around this island. When I get down in the dumps, I just think of what I have waiting for me when I get back, and I feel better.

"You're working too hard," he wrote. She knew he meant all the things she had been doing in the apartment in addition to working every day. "I want you to slow down and take care of yourself. I can tell by some of your letters that you aren't feeling well."

He was right. She had not been feeling well, still she felt driven to do more and more. No matter how much she accomplished in a day, she always felt she should have done more.

How she wished she could be as serene as Thelma. At first She thought Thelma just happened to be in a good mood each time she saw her, but as months went by, and Thelma was always calm and smiling, Jeanie knew there

CHAPTER THIRTEEN

was something different about her than anyone she had known before.

There was something different about Charles, too. The only time she had heard him speak in an angry tone was once when they had been talking about Hollywood stars. He said they were certainly not people to idolize. Jeanie was startled, but she realized their multiple marriages, wild parties, and drunkenness were certainly not lifestyles to emulate. The odd part was that Charles wasn't angry at the movie stars, but at the way they lived.

"I never heard anyone talk about God as comfortably as they do," she wrote to Kenny. "They talk like they really know Him. I believe in Him, but He feels so far away. I wish I could be like Thelma and Charles."

If there ever was a time she needed to feel close to God, it was now. Every time she read headlines or listened to the news fear clutched her stomach and made her knees feel weak. Why couldn't she be as calm and trusting as they were? Charles had a brother overseas and they didn't know where he was either. Though they were concerned and eager to know he was safe, they never seemed full of fear the way she was.

Maybe if she started going to their church it would help. She went with them to their church once, and she liked the informality and the warmth. "People sing from their hearts, not their hymnbooks," she wrote to Kenny.

She suggested that when he was home on furlough, they go there and maybe eventually join that church. After all, it was the same denomination. But he reminded her that their families had been in that branch of the denomination for three generations, and he was not about to break that tradition. "We'll talk about it when I come home," he promised.

133

When Jeanie went down to pay the rent the week of D-Day, Thelma invited her to have Sunday dinner with them. "Would you like to come to church with us?" she asked.

Jeanie eagerly accepted.

Again, Jeanie was favorably impressed by the way the people at this church worshiped. But she had that strange feeling again—of being on the outside looking in. She was an observer, not a participant.

It surprised her to see how the congregation lingered outside after the service and enjoyed talking with each other. They even talked about God! She had never heard anyone, but maybe Gram, talk about God once they were out of church.

Later at dinner, she enjoyed sitting at their table with little Elizabeth in her high chair, smiling just like her parents.

It was the first decent meal she had eaten in days, and when Charles passed the platter, she gratefully accepted a second helping of the delicious pot roast. She was rarely able to buy fresh meat. She saw the lines at the meat market on her way to work, but by the time she got back, she was able to get only bologna or an occasional soup bone and sometimes some chicken.

They talked about the invasion and agreed that it seemed like the tide of the war had turned. Charles said now was the time people needed to trust the Lord for the safety of their loved ones.

But back upstairs, even though Jeanie had heard all those comforting words, fear took its familiar place in the pit of her stomach. How she longed to be able to turn off her thoughts the way she could turned off the radio.

The Monday after D-Day, smiles were rare on the streetcar, and everyone seemed intent on his own business again. Headlines told of intense fighting.

Chapter Thirteen

If only she knew where Kenny was.

The Sunday after D-Day, June 11, Emma sat gently swinging on the porch swing, watching a robin tussle with an exceptionally elastic worm. It stretched so long that the robin almost lost his balance when it came out of the ground.

Ordinarily, Emma would have chuckled and would have smiled with satisfaction at the fast-growing tomato plants she could see through the wire garden fence. A gentle shower had turned the clay road up the hillside to a rich red brown and the air had that lovely after-rain fragrance.

But this afternoon she was oblivious to all that. Her thoughts were on the thousands of young men fighting in France. *Was Kenny one of them? Were any of her grandsons there?* She thought of their young faces and their strong, young bodies.

These days had been one long prayer for their protection, and now she realized another prayer was needed—one for strength and comfort for those who waited.

How she wished she could put her arms around Jeanie and comfort her. *O Lord, please let her hear from him soon.*

Day after day there was no letter from Kenny. Then June 12, Jeanie received a letter written May 31. She was happy to hear from him, but she still didn't know where he was.

Tension built to the point where she felt like crying most of the time. She didn't know what to pray, except, *Please keep him safe.*

Then a week later, she got the letter he wrote June 8. He was still in England!

"Well the big job is started," he'd written. "It's about time! It feels good to know we did our little part in our truck company. We've been pretty busy. I'll have plenty to tell you when I get home. I'm sending a message we each got from General Eisenhower. Keep it for me, will you?"

Jeanie unfolded the soiled paper. Printed in heavy black letters, at the top was "Supreme Headquarters, Allied Expeditionary Force."

She read:

> Soldiers, Sailors and Airmen of the Allied Expeditionary Force!
>
> You are about to embark upon the Great Crusade, toward which we have striven these many months. The eyes of the world are upon you. The hopes and prayers of liberty-loving people everywhere march with you. In company with our brave Allies and brothers-in-arms on other Fronts, you will bring about the destruction of the German war machine, the elimination of Nazi tyranny over the oppressed peoples of Europe, and security for ourselves in a free world.
>
> Your task will not be an easy one. Your enemy is well trained, well equipped and battle-hardened. He will fight savagely.
>
> But this is the year 1944! Much has happened since the Nazi triumphs of 1940–41. The United Nations have inflicted upon the Germans great defeats, in open battle, man-to-man. Our air offensive has seriously reduced their strength in the air and their capacity to wage war

CHAPTER THIRTEEN

on the ground. Our Home Fronts have given us an overwhelming superiority in weapons and munitions of war, and placed at our disposal great reserves of trained fighting men. The tide has turned! The free men of the world are marching together to Victory!

I have full confidence in your courage, devotion to duty and skill in battle. We will accept nothing less than full Victory!

Good Luck! And let us all beseech the blessing of Almighty God upon this great and noble undertaking.

It was signed, "Dwight D. Eisenhower."

The letter still clutched in her hand, Jeanie fell across her bed and sobbed until she fell asleep.

Early in June, news came that the Allied forces began operating from French airstrips. But right on the heels of that good news came reports of new weapons the Germans were launching against London. These small, jet-propelled pilotless planes, called V-1 rockets, carried the equivalent of a freight-car load of explosives and traveled at about 350 miles per hour. They were immediately dubbed "buzz bombs" because of the noise they made. Jeanie wondered what new terror this weapon would bring.

By the middle of June, all five of the Allied beachheads were linked—the British Juno, Sword, and Gold beachheads, with the US Utah and Omaha—to form a solid, fifty-mile front.

"At least Ray's still in the States," Jeanie wrote to Kenny. "He would have been in the thick of it on D-Day."

Soon after D-Day, Ray came home on furlough, wearing his lieutenant's uniform, and Jeanie saw him briefly when he came through Chicago on his way to Wisconsin. Vi and the little ones went to Wisconsin on the train to

137

spend most of the summer with Kenny's folks, so Vi was able to be with Ray.

The third Sunday in June, Lenore invited Jeanie to come home with her for dinner. Lenore's father also extended a hearty invitation.

They lived in a large, second-floor apartment not far from the church. Jeanie's heart ached when she met Lenore's mother, who was crippled with rheumatoid arthritis and rarely left their home.

That evening Jeanie had plenty to write to Kenny.

> You'd like Lenore. She's peppy, optimistic, and fun to be with—cute, too. Her parents were especially nice to me and told me I was welcome any Sunday I want to come.
>
> Her mother's hands are so crippled it hurt me to watch her try to help with dinner. It's amazing what she can accomplish.
>
> We went for a long walk through Humboldt Park, and I told Lenore how you and I used to walk there the summer before we were married. She asked questions and more questions, but I didn't mind. It's fun to tell her about how we met in high school, held hands in the corridors, and got scolded by the principal. At least I did! Remember how angry you were, because he had called me into the office and not you? You always wanted to protect me.
>
> I hope she meets a nice guy soon. Everyone's gone now, but after the war she's sure to meet someone.
>
> Oh, I'm going to start a Red Cross first-aid class with Lenore on Thursday night. I hope I'll never have to give first aid, but it won't hurt to learn how. Now that Vi and the kids are gone for the summer, I have a free evening.

CHAPTER THIRTEEN

That night, as Jeanie evaluated her day and wondered if she used it wisely, she decided that spending the day with Lenore had, indeed, been a wise use of time.

The third week of July, the Democrats held their convention in Chicago and nominated Franklin D. Roosevelt for his fourth term as president. Senator Harry S. Truman was chosen as his running mate.

The Republicans earlier nominated Thomas E. Dewey, governor of New York, for president, and John W. Bricker for vice president.

Jeanie wondered if it would be wise to change presidents in the midst of the war.

Fourteen

As the Chicago temperature climbed, and the old, black machines held yesterday's heat and added today's, Jeanie was glad she had decided to take her week's vacation the end of July.

It would be warm in Wisconsin, too, but a tremendous relief to have the temperature drop at night. The Concord Place apartment was horribly hot. The only way she could stand it was to move a little fan so it blew directly on her wherever she worked, ate, or slept.

It seemed strange to visit Gram in her little house, instead of the rooms that were home to her and Jeanie for seventeen years.

141

The second night Jeanie was home she wrote to Kenny,

I wish you could have seen Gram today. I had been visiting with Helen and ran back to Gram's house. When I opened the kitchen door, there she was scooping water up with a dustpan! You know her knees are stiff and she can't stoop, so she was standing, legs far apart, a lock of long, gray hair hanging down, and was scooping water into a pail with the dustpan. She had tried mopping and wringing, but I guess that was too slow to suit her.

I couldn't imagine what had happened. Of course she was startled when she saw me. (How do you not startle a deaf person?) But she recovered immediately and said, "Just look at this mess! I was filling the water pail and didn't want to stand and wait, so I sat down for a minute." (She doesn't have a sink. Just a faucet and water pail.) "I didn't remember the water was running until I felt my feet getting wet. What an old fool!"

She had to chuckle in spite of herself and let me take over and mop it up. I was glad she couldn't hear me laughing.

Of course, everyone wants to know where you are, but all I could tell them is that the last I heard, you were still in England.

A few nights later she wrote,

It's good to see Grace and Myrtle. Grace's husband is overseas and she's staying home for a while. Boy, Aunt Ella's house sure is lively again with Myrtle and her little ones at home.

Aunt Mamie and Uncle Al have a service flag in their front window with three stars on it now. I did write that Ruby joined the WACS, didn't I? We sure missed her this week.

142

CHAPTER FOURTEEN

Grace and I picked wild raspberries one day. You would have hated it, but I like to pick berries. We had such a great time talking. Remember how she always stuck up for the underdog when we were in school? She still does. She's not like me, so quick to criticize someone else's actions. I felt ashamed when she pointed out the possible reasons behind the things that bother me. I'm going to try to be more like her.

There were several letters waiting for Jeanie when she got home—all from England. In one, Kenny wrote that he was eager to get to France.

The next week there were no letters at all, and Jeanie reread his last letters each evening, thinking he must be on his way to France.

Then Monday, August 7, there was a V-mail from France.

"It's been some time since I had a chance to write, but I'm sure you'll understand when you read this letter," he wrote.

He printed "France" at the top of his July 27 letter. "We had a smooth trip over here. I saw the port of Cherbourgh and a few other beaches. They were really ripped up. Those poor guys!

"Don't worry about me. I'm just fine. Boy, will I be glad to get mail again."

There was another letter the next day. He said he liked France so far, but it was really hard to find his way around the highways, with all the signs in French. "The captain tried to teach us some French tonight, but I don't think I learned much."

"Well, at least he'll get to see a lot of France if he's driving a truck," Pat said at work the following noon.

Kate smiled. "Maybe you'll relax now that you know where he is."

143

As Long as I Have You

Jeanie nodded. She hadn't been aware how tense she was, even after she had found out Kenny was still in England after D-Day. "I guess I couldn't really settle down until I knew he was in France."

Pat said her two brothers in the Air Corps were still all right. But how could anyone know from day to day? Kate was dreading the day when her son Larry would be through with his training.

Spirits rose on August 15 with news of a huge Allied landing in southern France.

The Allies entered Paris on August 25, and some people thought the war was virtually over. But from what Jeanie read in the newspapers, it seemed there was a long way to go.

At least letters were reaching Kenny regularly now, and his were coming through in about ten days. He wrote that he lived for her letters.

Jeanie felt the same way, and one evening when she heard the song, "Love letters dear to my heart,/Keep us so near while apart," she was sure it had been written just for them. She asked Kenny if he had heard that song.

Once, he had written that, when he read her letters, he could just see what she was doing, to which she answered,

> Oh, I know what you mean about letters. When I read them, it's almost like you were talking to me. I never tire of hearing "I love you". If you told me a million times, it wouldn't be enough. It's over a year since we've seen each other, but do you know what I think? Remember how it was when you met Spike at the train station? You hadn't seen each other for over a year, and yet in a few minutes, it was like you had never been apart. I think that's the way it will be with us.

Chapter Fourteen

There's one difference, though. I don't see how we could ever take each other for granted after being so lonesome for each other for so long. I wonder if couples who have never had to be apart can possibly appreciate being together like those of us who are hurting so much.

It always took a while, after she finished writing to Kenny, to replace her loneliness with plans for the next day.

Plans—they were what kept her going. The way to cope, she decided, was to keep busy, to do so many things that she would literally drop with exhaustion at night.

Still, there was always the feeling that she hadn't done quite enough to improve herself, to help others, or to aid the war effort. It was as if some unseen force was urging her to do more and more and more. Yet, there were times she was so tired, she wanted to go to bed and stay there for a week. There had to be a balance between work and rest, but try as she would, she couldn't find it.

Fifteen

A wave of apprehension swept over Jeanie when the first dry leaves scudded along the sidewalks in September. *Another winter without Kenny? Another Christmas without him?* She couldn't even remember living without an aching heart. It was like being a little girl again, struggling with a heavy load of wood and telling herself, *You can make it. It's only a few more steps.* She always made it. But that had been a different kind of struggle—a different kind of weight. She wasn't at all sure she could carry this one much longer.

It didn't help to know that the Germans began launching an even more powerful rocket—the V-2. These rockets traveled at supersonic speeds that made their missles impossible to detect or shoot down. Of course, it was reassuring to know that the Allies established a solid front in Europe, but that cost many lives, and progress was painfully slow. Nor was there good news from the Pacific. As far as Jeanie could tell, the war in the Pacific hadn't reached a turning point. There appeared to be little hope of the war ending either in Europe or the Pacific in 1944.

Although Gen and Jeanie were much aware of the war, their Monday evenings together were the bright spots in Jeanie's weeks. After dinner, and when their bandage work at Judson Baptist Church was finished, the girls would write to their men—Gen sitting on her bottom bunk and Jeanie cross-legged on the top.

"Say hi! to Kenny," Gen would always tell her.

Jeanie would reply, " And you say hi! to Warren."

Warren was training to be a radioman in the naval air corps. The couple hoped to get married if he came home on leave before he was shipped overseas.

Those Monday-night letters to Kenny were usually the shortest, because she and Gen did more talking than writing.

September 27 Jeanie wrote to Kenny, "News flash! Gen and Warren are getting married Saturday night. She called me and said, 'Would you like to come to our wedding Saturday evening at seven?' Talk about an instant wedding. Her friend Ellie is going to be her only bridesmaid. They'll be married at Judson Baptist Church, of course."

Excitedly, Jeanie took the el down to the Loop, where she bought a crystal bowl overlaid with silver for Gen and Warren's wedding gift.

The night of the wedding, Jeanie wrote:

Oh, Kenny, I wish you could have seen Warren when Gen came down the aisle. I'll never forget the love in his eyes! Of course Gen was beautiful. She always is. She wore a powder blue suit that made her eyes look even more blue. It seemed like everyone was crying because

Chapter Fifteen

they know in a few days Warren will be shipped out to who-knows-where. People have good reason to cry at weddings these days.

It was fun telling Pat and Kate when Kenny wrote something special in one of his letters. Usually, he told her how many hours he had been on the road, how tired he was, and there were always welcomed assurances of his love. But now and then he'd tell her about some interesting, and sometimes heartwarming, episode. "There's a little French kid that hangs around here all the time," he once wrote. "We call him Chris. He's only about three. He's always first in the chow line, and when we got paid the other day, he even sweat out the pay line. We can't understand him, but he sure is cute and we're spoiling him rotten."

Another time he wrote about the company mascot, a rabbit named Lucky. "Some guy bought a black male to keep Lucky company, and someone else found three little wild ones, so we have five now. We'll soon have a rabbit farm instead of a truck company."

Another time he wrote,

> I just took a shower! We made portable showers and they work swell. And our captain bought a radio and hooked it up with loudspeakers so we can all hear it. It sure sounds swell to hear a radio again. Have you heard There'll Be Blue Birds over the White Cliffs of Dover? I like that. And I get choked up when I hear I'll Walk Alone. You said Uncle Roy called that your song. Baby, I know you'll walk alone. I never worry about you. Last

As Long as I Have You

night I heard Dick Haymes sing, I'll Get By as Long as I Have You. That's *my* song.

When Kenny got the letter about berry picking, he wrote,

> I'm sure glad you had a good time picking berries. I hated it. I never could get my pail full.
>
> I bet it seems odd when you get back in the city after being up there in the woods. I lay here and think about how I'll act when I get back. I guess everything will seem pretty different for a while. But I know a few things I won't have any trouble adjusting to! I miss you so much. All I want to do is get this war over and get home to you. You're all I ever want . . .

In the next letter he wrote,

> I slept on a cot for the first time since I hit France. We're living in big tents now, instead of pup tents—right in an apple orchard. The only trouble is that the apples are bitter. I think I've tried every tree and they're all alike. Last night I was sick as heck. Must have been from those darned apples.
>
> I think we've got more German vehicles back here than they have on the other side of the front. There are German jeeps, motor cycles, and trucks all over the place, and now German prisoners are working around here.

A few days later he wrote, "We're moving all the time now. When the front moves, we move. Now I get to go on longer trips. Don't worry if you don't get letters for a few days now and then, because it's pretty hard to write when I'm on a run."

CHAPTER FIFTEEN

Jeanie was glad he warned her because it was the last letter she got for a week.

"I just got back from a four-day trip," he wrote. "There were twenty letters waiting for me. I file 'em according to date and read 'em whenever I get a little time. You see why it gets pretty hard to answer your questions sometimes."

By the middle of September his brother Ray was fighting in France. Kenny wrote that he got a letter from him and wished he could get up to the front to see him. That letter, written September 14, was the last to arrive for days. *He certainly must be out on a long run*, she thought.

September 26, their second anniversary, Jeanie relived their wedding day, hour by hour. She was put on a special job, working with fuzzy, cotton yarn for a few days, and the lint was everywhere. It clung to her eyelashes, tickled her nose and made her sneeze—even got in her mouth. What a way to spend an anniversary! But where, she wondered, was Kenny spending it? Had he managed to get a leave and tried to find Ray at the front? She quickly put her mind back on wedding memories.

Kenny's birthday, September 29, came and went with no letter. October 1 and still no letter. Every night Jeanie would look for white spots in the mailbox holes as soon as she rounded the corner. If she saw white, she couldn't run across the street fast enough. But it was always letters from Gram or someone else. Still, she was happy to get them, and they helped her get through another night.

Her anxiety grew more each day, until she dreaded letter writing. Although she tried to conceal her concern for him, she wanted to scream, "Kenny! Where are you? Are you all right?" Countless times a day she whispered, "O Lord, keep him safe wherever he is!"

151

As Long as I Have You

Her prayers became even more urgent when, at work one day, she heard that Rose, one of the older ladies, had received word that her son was missing in action.

Then October 12, two days less than a month since the last letter, she flew across the street when she saw white spots. With trembling fingers, she pulled out a fat letter from Kenny! She tore it open right there and began to read it.

"I bet you've been thinking your little man broke his arm or something. Well, I didn't, but I just couldn't write. I've been on the road for over two weeks. There were four trucks besides mine. We had to report to one place, pick up a load, deliver it, report to another place, and so on, day after day. We drove practically day and night. I put on over 3000 miles, so you see I haven't been playing around. It takes time to load and unload too. We never knew what or when we'd eat next. We just bummed what we could from every mess hall as we went along."

The words blurred through tears of relief. She brushed them away with the back of her hand, being careful not to spot the letter. Then she ran upstairs to finish reading it.

"We've got it made here now. We took over a German camp and we're in barracks. They really had a nice setup. Don't worry about me. I've got a good job.

"Remember I said I wanted to see Paris? Well I've been through Paris five times in the last two weeks! I never did get any time to run around or to shop, though.

"The guys are razzing me about being twenty-one. They say I can talk with the men now.

"I didn't forget our anniversary. Even though the time was different, I thought about what we were doing on our wedding day, hour by hour. I thought, too, about what we'll

CHAPTER FIFTEEN

say when we first see each other. All I know is that it will be the happiest day of my life."

Before Jeanie could tell Thelma about the letter and call Vi, she had to cry out all the accumulated tension and wanted to thank God for keeping him safe.

In his next letter Kenny, wrote,

> Man! I just missed seeing Ray. He wrote that he had been wounded—not bad: got nicked in the rear end and was in the hospital. I could have seen him one of those times I was in Paris, but I didn't know he was there. That darn letter took two weeks to get to me! Boy, he'll never hear the end of that—getting a purple heart for a nick in the butt!
>
> I'm glad you and Vi get along so well and that you have fun with the kids. Just wait till we get our Kent and Joannie. It seems as though they are real, instead of just talk. That will be another one of your big days—when we get our first little one. It doesn't make any difference to me which one comes first; how about you?

One evening early in October, when Jeanie went to visit Vi and Art, Vi handed Jeanie a letter from Ray.

"Three pages, on both sides. That's the longest letter he's ever written," Vi said. "He's in the hospital again so he has time to write."

"Wounded again?" Jeanie scooped up little Bobby on her lap and held the letter at arm's length, so he couldn't grab it.

"No. He has an infection. I'll let you read about it."

Jeanie tried to ignore the giggles and screams of the other three little ones and read, "We've moved far and fast, but we can't write about anything until at least fourteen days

153

As Long as I Have You

after it happens. I haven't had a chance to tell you about when we came into Paris. When we came in, the people flocked the streets and tried to hang on the trucks. Some had to kiss you, and being in the cab, I got a lot of that. We had all we could do to get the truck down the street. We stayed three days, and people flocked around that park like it was a zoo and we were the monkeys. We had to rope off an area so we could eat."

Ray went on to tell how the Belgian people treated them like kings. "They brought us coffee and bread and butter, and whenever possible, they let us use their barns and garages for the night."

He told about some close calls when they were hitting the Siegfried line. Once he was knocked on his face by a mortar shell. "It tore out the seat of my pants, and shrapnel cut lightly into the left rear cheek. The same shell wounded two others and killed my radio man by my side."

Jeanie stopped reading and said, "Kenny wrote about Ray getting hit in the rear, but I didn't know his radio man was killed right beside him!" She read on: "Now I have an infection in my right ankle, and I'm in France. By the time you get this, I'll be back in my unit.

"I've done things I never thought I'd do—like going twenty-two days without taking off my clothes or bathing."

Little Bobby squirmed and tried to reach the letter. "Come here you little rascal!" Vi said and took him so Jeanie could read in peace.

On the last page she read, "God sure has been with me since I've been in action. I start each day with a prayer and end each day with one and usually get in two or three during the day as things get tough. I'm a very firm believer in prayer and a reformed person altogether."

Chapter Fifteen

Jeanie blinked back tears, folded the letter and handed it to Vi. "We can only imagine what he has seen and experienced. It makes me more grateful than ever that Kenny's a truck driver."

Emma was walking through the backyard with a basket of wood chips for starting a fire, when Helen came back from the mailbox. She waved a letter, and Emma waited.

Emma scanned the return address. "My goodness! A letter from Kenny. I'll bring it over in a little while," she promised, heading for her little house. She wanted to take her time reading it.

Still in her sweater, she cut off the end of the envelope and sat down in her rocker. She read, her lips forming the letters,

Dear Gram,
    It's about time I write to you. I know Jeanie tells you what's going on with me, but I thought you'd like to get a letter once. "I'm fine. I've got a good job driving a truck behind the lines. Don't worry about me. I'm not in any real danger. Wish you could see this country. You'd love it. So far, I haven't seen a lot of mountains, but once we get pushing those Germans back, I'll get into mountain country.
    "Well, election day is coming up soon. I don't know how you feel, but I sure hope Roosevelt gets in again.
    "I hope you're feeling well. I know you keep working all the time. Pretty soon I'll dig out those heavy socks you knit for me. It's gets pretty cold at night, even though

it's only October. Guess we'll be in for some cold this winter if we get into the mountains. We keep moving right behind the front.

"Don't worry about Jeanie, either. I'm sure proud of the way she's holding our little home for me. As long as I have her, I can get through most anything.

"Pray for my brother Ray. He's with the 4th Infantry Division and has been wounded once all ready. It was nothing serious, thank God.

"I hope you'll have some fresh coffee *kuchen* ready when I get back!

Love, Kenny

Emma smiled and put the letter back in its envelope. That dear boy. "Thank you for keeping him behind the lines," she whispered as she took the letter to Helen.

The letter Jeanie received on Halloween had been written October 23. Kenny was in a low mood. He admitted he had counted on the war being over before the first of the year. Now that it was apparent it would go on a lot longer, the guys were depressed. "Even though it looks like it will be a while before this war is over, most of the talk is about what we'll do when it ends—except sometimes we talk sports. Everyone wants to see the football scores when the *Stars and Stripes* comes out."

Jeanie didn't stay up late enough to get the November 7 election results, but the next morning, when she heard the news that Roosevelt had won again, she sighed in relief.

CHAPTER FIFTEEN

Days dragged by uneventfully until on the streetcar one November morning, Jeanie had the feeling someone was watching her. When she glanced up, her eyes met those of a handsome, well-dressed businessman, sitting across from her on the opposite side-seat by the rear door. He quickly dropped his eyes.

At California Avenue Jeanie got up to stand by the door, and the man did too. She wasn't surprised, because she had seen him before and knew he changed streetcars at that corner.

As they were waiting for the California Avenue car, she found him looking at her again, only this time he smiled instead of shifting his gaze.

Several times during the day she remembered that smile.

The next morning there wasn't a single empty seat on the streetcar, and the same good-looking man moved over to make room for her on a side seat. She gave him a brief thank-you smile, but neither of them said a word.

She didn't see him for a few days, but when she did, it was obvious he had saved a seat for her by taking up extra space.

He nodded and smiled when she murmured her thanks, but he didn't try to start a conversation.

It annoyed her when she recalled the incident later in the day. Why should she even think about it?

Then one day as Jeanie was huddled close to a building in the icy wind, waiting for the California Avenue car, he walked over and stood so he would protect her from the wind. "There, does that help a bit?" he asked in a deep mellow voice.

She nodded gratefully but turned away when he kept looking at her.

157

As Long as I Have You

"I'm sorry if I make you uncomfortable," he said, "but you are awfully easy to look at, you know!"

Several times that day Jeanie was angry with herself for allowing that scene to keep coming back in her mind.

That evening Kenny's letter swept away all thoughts of the handsome stranger.

His letter disturbed her, though, because he wrote that he sometimes felt the war was forgotten back home in the States. Jeanie assured him that wasn't true. "It seems everywhere I look there's a billboard or a poster with old Uncle Sam pointing his finger at me saying, "Uncle Sam wants *you!*" she wrote. "And bond rallies featuring Hollywood stars are advertised all the time. As far as I can see, people are doing everything they can to help end this war as soon as possible. Oh, I've read about people hoarding scarce items, and I guess there are some black-market operations, but you know there are always people who try to make a quick buck wherever they can. I don't know what you're hearing that makes you think the general public doesn't care."

Christmas decorations appeared in store windows, and Jeanie wondered how she would get through another Christmas without Kenny.

The friendly man on the streetcar continued to save a seat for her whenever she caught the 7:35 car. When she missed it, she had to run like crazy so she could punch in at eight. One morning she was coming in the north door and saw the spool boy back by the time clock. She waved, and he punched her in. After that, she was sure to catch the 7:35 streetcar and told herself it had nothing to do with the friendly man on that car.

CHAPTER FIFTEEN

One morning when she smiled her thanks and sat down in the saved seat, he smiled back and asked, "Where do you work?"

Jeanie told him, proudly adding that she worked on parachute cords. Though she didn't ask him, he told her where he worked, assuring her it too, was essential war work.

"But that's not why I'm not in service," he quickly added. "I was classed 4-F because I have a bad heart—something I was born with." He shrugged. "Doesn't bother me with the type of work I do."

When she didn't answer, he said, "I wanted you to know so you wouldn't think I was a draft dodger. By the way, my name is Tony."

"Jeanie," she said in return. "My husband's in Europe, in the Quartermaster Corps," she added quickly.

"Does that keep him behind the lines?"

Jeanie nodded. "I'm sure glad he isn't in the infantry, like his brother."

Again, she was angry at herself for thinking about their conversation several times during the day. Those eyes! They were a deep, soft brown.

December 1 Jeanie got the letter Kenny had written November 22.

Ray got wounded again. He's back in the hospital in Paris. He got hit in the head with a dud—that's a shell that didn't go off. Boy! Is he lucky that thing wasn't a live one. He can't be hurt too bad. He was able to write to me. I'm hoping to go and see him day after tomorrow, if everything works out and I can get a weekend pass. Sure hope it does. We haven't seen each other for over two years.

159

As Long as I Have You

She didn't get another letter for more than a week. On November 26 he wrote,

> I'm back again, Baby, and feeling fine. I got to see Ray, and we had a really long talk. I spent two full days with him. He's doing all right. Had a concussion and a cut on his head. The nurse told me they're keeping him for a good rest before he goes back to the front again.
>
> I slept in a real bed with sheets, right in the hospital. Ain't that something! They even served me breakfast. For a while, I forgot I was in the army. They sure treated me well.
>
> I caught one of our trucks yesterday and got back here about two in the morning, slept till noon, went out on a run this afternoon, and here I am, writing to my one and only. It sure was good to see Ray. He hasn't changed a bit. Tell Vi.

December 17 Jeanie heard distressing news. The Germans had broken through the Allied lines in the Ardennes Forest.

Monday morning when Jeanie got on the streetcar she saw frightening newspaper headlines. Our boys were really in trouble. With a groan, she sat down next to Tony and pointed to the headline on his newspaper. "What's happening? It scares me!"

Tony shook his head. "Looks like the Germans are pouring on everything they have right now, but it's probably a last-ditch stand. Don't worry. They can't hold out long. Doesn't seem like they have any air force left."

When they got on the next streetcar at California, Tony was right behind her and whispered close to her ear, "Don't

160

CHAPTER FIFTEEN

worry. They don't have what it takes anymore. Our guys will lick 'em."

She thought of his kind remark several times that day, as well as that warm smile he flashed at her when she got on the streetcar every morning, and she was angry with herself every time she remembered them.

Sixteen

Again, it was time to go home for Christmas. The train to Wisconsin—an ancient one with a stove in the corner—was more crowded than ever.

"Either I'm growing, or Gram is shrinking," Jeanie wrote to Kenny her first evening home. "I don't think I'm growing!"

But the children certainly were! Baby Gene was over two now, and Jeanie loved to hear him talk. Of course Arne had a lot to tell her.

Jeanie tried to capture the Christmas spirit, but her heart was like lead. News of the war continued to be bad. Thousands of Allied troops were cut off, and the fighting was furious. Was Ray back in it? Where was Kenny?

Thelma had promised to forward any early letters from Kenny, but not a single one came.

After the Christmas Eve children's program at church, Roy set up Gram's tree, and Jeanie took out the old ornaments. Gram watched her for a while, telling her the history of some of them. Then she said, "Hand me my comb." She chuckled, "I'm too lazy to get up."

Jeanie took the big, ivory comb out of the metal comb holder that hung below the washstand mirror and handed Gram the comb.

Out of the corner of her eye, Jeanie watched Gram take out the amber hairpins, comb through her hair, braid it, and as Jeanie had seen her do a thousand times before, take the loose hairs from the comb and wind them around the end of her braid to secure it.

Gram yawned and said, "Well, I can't keep my eyes open any longer. It's way past my bedtime."

Her warm hug said more to Jeanie than anything else she might have spoken.

Slowly Emma undressed, thinking she should have made an effort to stay up with Jeanie and tried to cheer her somehow. But Jeanie hadn't made any attempt all evening to talk with her. Maybe she wanted to be alone to remember happier Christmases.

But as Emma pulled her feet into bed, she knew the truth was that she couldn't bear one more minute of that sad little face. "Lord," she whispered, "you know how close I've been to crying all evening. It wouldn't help for her to see *me* cry—would it?"

It had been a long time since she had been able to bend her stiff knees to kneel and pray, but she knew the Lord understood. The Lord knew. "Father," she continued, her hands clasped under her pillow to keep them warm, "I try to understand what I read in the papers about the war, but I can't put it all together. All those names! I sure do know

Chapter Sixteen

the news is bad, and I can see the worry on everyone's face." Emma choked back a sob. "So many people hurting, Lord. Not only in this country, but also the innocent people who didn't ask for this war. Please bring this awful war to an end, and send the troops home."

How many times had she prayed that prayer, she wondered. "Father, I don't understand why it's taking so long, but I trust you no matter what."

Tired . . . so tired. The familiar words, "Come unto me, all ye that labor and are heavy laden, and I will give you rest," came to her, and she repeated them. "I trust you. . . . I trust you . . . ," she murmured. Then, in the midst of her exhaustion, came the Lord's sweet presence.

"Thank you, Jesus!" she sighed, and for the first time that evening, she was aware of the fragrance of the balsam tree.

She pulled the covers up over her shoulders. "Comfort Jeanie, O Lord . . . comfort Jeanie. . . ."

Quiet. So quiet. Silent night, Jeanie thought. No radio in Gram's house. Only the wind and the crackle of the fire in the heater stove.

Again, it was as if she were standing aside, watching herself go through the motions of trimming the tree. She didn't feel like crying. She didn't feel anything but empty tonight. In a way, she wished she could feel something beside this detached numbness.

When she went over to the big house to go to bed, she listened to the news on the radio awhile with Roy and Helen as they trimmed their tree. She couldn't get it all clear in her mind, but she did know the Allied troops were still isolated in Bastogne.

Helen and Roy tried to make small talk, and she knew they were hurting for her.

Quietly she climbed the stairs. *Surely*, Jeanie thought as she shivered in the icy bed, *this will go down in history as the most miserable Christmas Eve of our lives.*

❧

It was almost a relief to be back in her little attic rooms, where she didn't have to pretend she was all right. It was easier to just work, eat, sleep, and work some more.

The first morning she got on the streetcar, there was Tony with his smile and kind brown eyes. She felt warmed, even happy, when he said, "Where *were* you! I thought something happened to you."

She told him about her visit home, and he said, "I wish you had told me you were going."

At work her thoughts were in turmoil. Why should Tony care about her? He certainly knew she was married. Had she led him on? No, she reasoned. It was perfectly natural to talk to someone you rode with day after day. But then, why did it bother her so much that she looked forward to his smiles—that warm feeling when she sat next to him?

The first week in January, the Germans launched another heavy attack on Bastogne. Never had days been darker.

One day there were two letters from Kenny. One had been written, on Christmas Eve and the other Christmas Day. "It's Christmas Eve again. My second one overseas. I just got back from our shelter. We had some very unwelcome visitors. Last night was even worse. We sang Christmas carols until the all-clear sounded. I have to go out on a run at six tomorrow morning. They're having turkey here, but I'll have K-rations. I hope they save some for us guys who are out. I know this Christmas must have been rough for you too, but next year we'll be together for sure."

December 26 he wrote, "Well, a bunch of us got back late Christmas night, and the cooks had saved us some turkey. It sure was good. I didn't mind working. Anything to help end this war. Guess what! I had a package from you waiting for me. Right on Christmas day! The candy sure is good. I laughed when I saw the slippers, but they're all right! Sure beats wearing GI boots around the barracks. I got another Christmas present; a good conduct medal and a driver's medal. I can do without a Purple Heart."

In his next letter, he wrote that he had a letter from Ray, saying he was headed back to the front again. Jeanie felt a cold chill.

January 10 there was good news. The Germans had been defeated in Bastogne. Almost everyone on the streetcar was smiling, including Tony. When they changed cars at California, he grinned and gave Jeanie a quick, one-armed hug.

All morning, Jeanie's thoughts went back to that brief physical contact. How she yearned to be held in strong arms.

That noon, Kate stretched out her tired legs, unfolded her lunch bag, and said, "Well, what are you up to these days?"

Before Jeanie could answer, Pat interrupted, "Just last night I was telling a friend about you—how you make the days count, instead of sitting around feeling sorry for yourself."

167

She went on to tell about some young women who were doing little but crying and worrying. Jeanie was relieved that she didn't have to answer Kate's question.

That evening after she had written to Kenny, she sat, pencil in hand, trying to make a list of things to do. The desire to cling to her resolve to make each day count was still there, but it was like trying to hold on to a slippery rope. How long was it since she felt enthusiastic about something? It was easier to curl up and feel sad—and to think about Tony's warm smile.

The paper was still blank when Jeanie went to bed.

Seventeen

January 12, Pat's eyes were swollen, her lovely skin blotchy. She sobbed out the news. Her oldest brother had been killed in action.

All Jeanie could do was hold her close and cry with her.

> I'm crying for both of us, for Pat and her family and for myself, because I've lost another friend. She's going to Dallas to stay with her sister-in-law and nephew—at least for a while. We were never close like Margie and I, but I'll miss her. Now there's just Kate and me. I like Kate a lot, and even though she's older, we get along fine. Her son's in France, and she's terribly concerned about him. Of course, now that the Battle of the Bulge is over, she'll rest a bit easier.

Winter dragged on and on. If the weather was really bad on a Monday, Jeanie would not go to Gen's. She was glad she took the first-aid course in good weather. It was good to be home and warm on cold, bleak nights, even though she still had little enthusiasm about anything. She worked each day, saved money, faithfully wrote letters to Kenny, Gram, and many others, babysat with Elizabeth, helped Vi now and then, rolled bandages, and kept her clothes and house clean. Still there was always the nagging guilt that she didn't do enough. The only bright spot in her days were Kenny's letters.

> We have a radio again. I don't know what happened to the one we had last fall, but we haven't heard music for months. Last night I heard Sammy Kaye. Man! That sounded good. That crazy "Chickery Chick" song was going in my mind all day. It's silly, but it's good to hear something besides war songs. Have you heard Perry Como sing, Till the End of Time? When you do, just pretend I'm singing it to you, 'cause that's just the way I feel about you. I've just about worn your pictures out looking at them.

On Janury 12 he wrote, "I got twenty-four letters last night, and every one was dated in November. Vi sent a picture of the kids. Boy, have they changed. They sure are cute.

"It's so much easier to write letters when I get them. When I read your letters, I can just picture what you write about, especially if you write about places I know. I guess it's hard for you to picture what I'm doing. Maybe the snapshots help a little. When I get home, you can ask me all about things and I'll try to answer all your questions."

"When I get home!" What beautiful words.

Then day after day, no letters. Meanwhile, Jeanie reread his most recent letters before going to bed.

The "Big Three"—Roosevelt, Churchill, and Stalin—met in Yalta to discuss problems of the postwar world. How,

CHAPTER SEVENTEEN

Jeanie wondered, could mere human beings make such momentous decisions?

Ten days and still no letter.

"You look so sad." Tony remarked one morning on the streetcar.

"No letters," she told him.

"I'm sorry." He squeezed her arm.

When she got off at Armitage, she glanced back at him. The warmth in his brown eyes stayed with her all morning.

News came that General MacArthur's troops had landed on Luzon in the Philippines, and February 7 MacArthur himself returned to Manila. This sounded like real progress.

Kenny's letter of January 24 came February 8. He had been on the road almost constantly. "The war here is really looking good. The Russians are sure on the move, and the last I heard, our troops were ninety-six miles from Berlin.

"Sure wish I'd get some mail. I haven't had a letter for ten days."

How frustrating it was to write every day, knowing Kenny was still without letters.

Three days later, he wrote that the mail came through and he got letters written in January, but received only a few written in December.

I got the package from Vi with the popcorn, too. Boy, did we have a feast! I popped it in my mess kit over our stove and dumped it in a steel helmet. Bill Cannon helped me eat it 'cause my buddy, Miller, wasn't here. That's the first popcorn I've had since I left Oregon. Gee, that's almost two and half years ago.

We've moved again and we're living in tents. Sure miss our water facilities, but at least we have electric lights. I've been in Holland and Belgium over and over.

171

A Belgian lady did my laundry last week just for some soap. They don't have any soap!

You asked about my truck. Well, it's a five-ton truck, but it's called a two-and-a-half-ton six-by-six. Two-and a-half tons is supposed to be the maximum load, but I've hauled as much as eight tons already.

You know what I wish I had right now? A glass of milk. I haven't had milk, except canned milk they use in cooking, since I've been overseas. That's a year and a half. But nice weather is coming and then things will really get rolling. This war can't last too much longer.

Baby, there were tear stains on one letter. I know just how you felt if you broke down while you were writing. I get so lonesome for you when I'm writing, I don't know what to do. But I think you're overtired. Don't push yourself so hard. Hang on! When these flooded rivers go down, watch our smoke.

That evening, she felt less pressure to accomplish more.

The third week in March Jeanie understood what Kenny had been looking forward to. The newspapers called the attack on German cities the most intensive air attack in history, and now troops had crossed the Rhine river at Remagen.

"Oh, Kate, it won't be long," Jeanie assured her, pulling up a stool and opening her lunch bag. "Can you imagine how we'll feel when the war is over in Europe?"

Kate sighed. "Yes, but then we'll be holding our breath for fear the guys will be sent to the Pacific."

"Oh, it's going to end there, too. I read that medium bombers are within reach of all Japan, now that we have air bases on Iwo Jima."

CHAPTER SEVENTEEN

Kate nodded and blinked back tears. "You're good for me, Jeanie. You're so optimistic, and I'm always looking on the dark side."

For the third time, the daffodils bloomed by the fence and their beauty made Jeanie's heart ache with longing to share spring with Kenny.

"I don't understand," she confided to Kate. "Instead of feeling happy when I see the flowers blooming and the trees budding, it hurts."

Kate didn't answer for a moment. She brushed some lint from her navy blue apron and nodded. "I know what you mean. It's like at Christmas when we're supposed to be happy, and instead we feel more sad then ever."

On the way home from work April 12, Jeanie remembered that it was her cousin Marilyn's twelfth birthday, and she hadn't sent a card. As usual, Jeanie turned on the radio but was barely aware of it as she went to wash her hands. Suddenly she heard an empty crackle—as if the station had gone off the air. In a moment a voice said, "We interrupt this program to bring you a special bulletin from CBS World News. A press association has just announced that President Roosevelt is dead. All that has been received is that bare announcement. There are no further details as yet, but CBS World News will return to the air in just a few minutes with more information as it is received in our New York headquarters."

No! Oh no! There must be some mistake. Not our *president*!

Jeanie raced downstairs to tell Thelma to turn on her radio, but no one was home.

173

As Long as I Have You

Back upstairs, she learned from her own radio that the President had died at Warm Springs, Georgia, of a cerebral hemorrhage. He was sixty-three.

"I just can't believe it!" Jeanie wrote Kenny that night. "President Roosevelt is dead! I know you must have heard, but I just have to write about it. I'm stunned. I stood out on our back porch and let the tears roll down as if I was joining the whole city—the whole country—in mourning. I felt so safe when he was reelected. This Harry Truman, who is he, anyhow? We had better pray that he knows what he's doing."

Before she went to bed, she heard that Harry S. Truman had been sworn in as president.

When Jeanie turned on the radio after work the next day, a reporter was telling how President Roosevelt's flag-draped bronze casket had been taken by hearse to the Warm Springs railroad station that morning. He said the streets were lined with troops from nearby Fort Benning, standing shoulder to shoulder to present arms. The hearse was followed by the Fort Benning Army Band and a hundred infantrymen armed with carbines. The colors of each company carried black streamers.

Tears spilled down Jeanie's cheeks as she sat in the rocker and listened.

He told how the casket was placed in the last car at the railroad station, behind a large window so it could be seen as the train passed.

People crowded the stations, he said. In one depot in South Carolina, as some Boy Scouts sang "Onward Christian Soldiers," the crowd around them joined in; then people a block away took up the singing until that singing spread through the whole town and on to the next.

174

CHAPTER SEVENTEEN

Saturday, Jeanie kept the radio on all day as she worked, cried, and prayed.

She heard how the President's casket was loaded on a black-draped caisson drawn by six white horses. The US Marine Band played Chopin's "Funeral March" and soldiers stood at attention at six-foot intervals along the way to the White House. The reporter said the whole procession was over two miles long and took over an hour to pass any given point. At one point, twenty-four huge bombers roared low over the line of march and past the White House.

That evening, Jeanie heard that about two hundred people crowded into the East Room of the White House for a service conducted by an Episcopal bishop.

Jeanie pictured the closed casket in the East Room between the portraits of George and Martha Washington, and pictured, too, the six servicemen standing at attention. She could also imagine Eleanor Roosevelt walking in, holding her son Elliott's arm.

Sunday evening the story continued. The train carrying the casket left Washington Saturday night for Hyde Park. At Hyde Park, about three hundred people gathered in the rose garden by the open grave, and the twenty-one-gun salute echoed across the Hudson, announcing the procession's arrival. Eight servicemen carried the coffin, and as they strained under its weight, two officers jumped up to assist them.

Dr. Anthony of St James Church read the committal words from the *Book of Common Prayer,* and the coffin was lowered into the ground. "West Point cadets fired three volleys," the reporter said. His voice was shaky as he continued, "Then came the saddest sound in the world—a bugler playing taps. My fellow Americans, the President is at rest."

The next morning on the streetcar, Tony sat close enough so their shoulders touched. He reached for her hand and she could feel the energy flowing between them.

"It's hard to believe, isn't it?" he said.

She nodded. She had wanted to turn and cry on his shoulder.

Later, when she remembered that feeling, she hated herself for wanting to be in Tony's arms. What was happening to her? The terrible attraction for Tony drew her like iron filings to a magnet. Never had she felt such conflict.

But I love Kenny! she protested in anguish. *How can I feel so attracted to a man I don't even know?*

Around and around her thoughts circled. One minute she was convinced she was not doing anything wrong, telling herself she was simply sitting and talking with a man on a streetcar and that he held her hand that morning simply because he knew she was sad. The next minute she would see herself eager to catch that streetcar every morning, drinking in Tony's wonderful, loving smile and feeling that warmth, that energy flowing between them.

Even worse, she began to wonder what it would be like if he kissed her.

She shook her head to rid herself of the mental images and told herself to think of Kenny.

Kenny . . . dear, funny, blue-eyed, loving Kenny.

There was a letter when she got home. She tore it open and flopped across the bed to read it.

"I know there's a lot of stuff going on with the wives," Kenny wrote. "A couple guys I know got Dear John letters. But Baby, I never worry about you. Nothing could ever tear us apart. You're all I ever want, and I know you feel the same."

Jeanie turned and sobbed into her pillow.

Eighteen

On Sunday, Lenore again invited Jeanie for dinner. It was a pleasant day as far as the conversation and bright spring weather were concerned, but Jeanie had that disturbing outside-looking-in feeling all day.

They took a long walk and stopped at a drugstore for a Coke. They talked a few minutes, and then Lenore snapped her fingers in Jeanie's face. "Hey there! Where are you? What's the matter with you?"

Instantly Jeanie came alert. "Oh, I'm sorry. I guess I'm in never-never land today." For one moment, she was tempted to tell Lenore all about Tony. But how could she? Lenore would never do anything so terrible.

She couldn't tell Thelma, either. She didn't want anyone to know how wicked she was.

That night, she resolved to leave for work earlier the next morning so she would not meet Tony. *Good-bye wonderful brown eyes. Good-bye beautiful smile. Good-bye warm, lovely feeling. I love Kenny. I don't need you!*

But the next morning, she found herself on the usual streetcar and loving the way Tony's eyes lighted up when he saw her in the red-and-white striped dress that accentuated her slim figure.

The streetcar was so crowded he wasn't able to find a seat even for himself, but stood waiting for her near the door.

"I'm sorry I couldn't get a seat for you. I know you have to stand all day at work."

She assured him she didn't mind and lost herself in the warmth that enveloped her as he clasped her hand.

He leaned close to her ear. "I have something to tell you."

She looked up at him and melted at the intensity of his gaze.

"I'm going to be transferred soon—down south on Cicero Avenue."

Her heart gave a jolt. What could she say?

As they waited for the next streetcar, Tony hovered close. "I tried to get out of it. I can't stand to think of not seeing you anymore."

She faced him squarely. "It's best this way. You know I'm married."

"Jeanie, . . . " he hesitated, looking off into Humboldt Park. "I'm married too. And I love my wife."

She caught her breath. *Why am I shocked?* she wondered. She shook her head and a sob caught in her throat. "I don't understand. I love my husband too. How can we love them and still feel like this?"

"Just because a person walks up to an altar and takes a vow, doesn't mean there still won't be attractions to someone else," Tony said softly.

"I just never thought that I . . ."

CHAPTER EIGHTEEN

"I know. It's the first time for me, too. Gee, I wouldn't want it to get out of hand. I'd never want to hurt you. You are so . . . so special."

They boarded the next car and stood close, but neither of them spoke. As they came near her stop, he gave her hand a quick squeeze and she got off the car without even looking at him.

A storm raged in her mind throughout the day. One second she was glad Tony was being transferred, the next she wondered how she could go on without the infusion of life his smile gave her each morning. One thing she knew, she could never tell anyone she did something so terrible.

That evening she was almost glad there was no letter from Kenny. She couldn't bear to read his trusting, loving words tonight.

Housework, sewing, the news broadcasts—nothing mattered. In an emotional fog, she took a long walk, bathed, and went to bed feeling too guilty even to try to pray.

That night she dreamed that she was in deep water, trying to kick her feet and get to the top, but no matter how hard she tried, the surface seemed miles above her. Her heart was thumping when she opened her eyes to the daylight.

"I'll be starting at the new location Monday," Tony said, holding her hand tightly as they sat side by side.

She simply nodded. *Three more days!* Friday would be the last day she would see him.

"Are you sorry—about us?" he asked.

She closed her eyes and groaned. "Ask me an easy one!" she said with a little, heartsick laugh.

The rest of the week, she accomplished virtually nothing at home and hated herself even more. What happened to all her fine resolutions to make the best possible use of her time? *Flirting with another man!* She wanted to die.

Friday she wore the red-and-white striped dress again.

"I know so little about you," she said when she settled herself beside him on the side seat.

He groaned. "I wish we could take off and walk for hours."

Jeanie followed his gaze to the spring green park. What if she offered to take the day off?

"Man," he said again, "I'd like to take the day off. . . ."

Slowly, deliberately, she shook her head. "I couldn't live with that. I can hardly live with. . . ."

"Don't! Oh, Jeanie, don't hate yourself! We haven't done anything wrong."

Oh, how she wanted to believe that.

At California and North he said, "Let's walk down the street a little way. Too many eyes here." There was no street-car coming, so they walked south on California Avenue. He pulled her into an entryway. "Jeanie, I just want to kiss you good-bye."

She didn't have time to answer.

His kiss was everything she'd imagined—sky rockets, the whole thing. Then, they were both were crying.

"D——!" he said, when he heard the streetcar. He grabbed her hand and they ran to catch it.

She was trembling so violently she was sure people could see it.

He leaned close just before she got to her corner. "Jeanie, be careful. You're so open and trusting."

She nodded. She wanted to say so much, but the words couldn't get past the lump in her throat.

One last look. One last zing of that wonderful energy.

She stumbled down the street as blindly as she did over two years ago when Kenny had stood waiting for the bus the day he was inducted.

Chapter Eighteen

But this time, she had guilt to cope with—suffocating guilt.

Although Emma heard the initial news of President Roosevelt's death from Helen, she gleaned the rest of the details from the newspaper. Watching for the mailman became a daily event for Emma, unless she happened to be visiting one of "the girls," as she still called her daughters and daughters-in-law. Because her little house afforded a better view of the road to the west than had her rooms in the old house, she watched for his car every forenoon.

Of course, Roy had no time to read the paper until evening, and Helen seemed to be in no hurry, so Emma kept the paper at her house to read in daylight. Even though she had good electric lights, it was easier for her to read in daylight.

Unlike those who were caught up in shock and grief and clung to every detail of the president's funeral, Emma's thoughts and concern were for President Truman. *What is it like to be suddenly thrust into this situation?* If what she read was true, vice presidents were not well informed. *Poor man! Poor man!*

Whenever she thought of him, she prayed God would grant him wisdom, physical strength—everything he would need.

But beyond the trauma of President Roosevelt's death, Emma felt an uneasiness about Jeanie. She had no idea what it was or why she felt so unsettled, but she knew the Lord

181

did. *Lord, you know what's wrong. Help her through whatever it is she is struggling with.*

Over and over that awareness came and refused to leave until she had prayed.

Ah, but who could be troubled long these days with the war news looking so good and with spring buds bursting on the trees. A United States Army unit had made contact with a Soviet Force—East had met West. Surely Germany would not hold out long now.

Then came the day Emma unfolded the *Milwaukee Journal* and read the most shocking news of her life; US forces had captured Dachau concentration camp and had freed thirty-two-thousand prisoners.

More details of the horrors unfolded as days went by. *How could this have happened? Why didn't the German people stop it? Did they know and simply were powerless to stop it? What agony! Only Satan himself could inspire such hideous atrocities.*

She clipped the dry stalks from the peonies, careful not to injure the new sprouts. Other years the very sight of new life flooded her with joy, but this year the sharp contrast of their beauty with the war horrors brought pain.

Jeanie lost no time opening Kenny's letters and devouring them whenever they came, but it was later, after she read them, that her conscience plagued her. Like the night she read, "Darling, I miss you so much that I hate to think about it 'cause it makes me feel as though my heart's not going to beat again, unless I can be with you. You know how that feels. If I lost you, I'd feel like a jeweler with his

CHAPTER EIGHTEEN

eyesight gone. But it won't be long, Baby. Things are really moving here."

Wow! What a letter for a guy who hated English classes and writing.

"Signing off to the best wife on earth," he wrote. *If he only knew.*

A few days later, he wrote that Gram had sent him another pair of hand-knit socks. "That little package meant more to me than lots of other packages I've received. Even though it's getting warmer here, I put them right on and they sure feel good tonight."

How dear of Gram. There was no doubt Kenny held a special place in her heart.

"Everyone writes and tells me how well you're doing—working hard, helping people, saving money, not complaining. I know all that, but it's sure nice to hear it from others," Kenny wrote.

How welcome that praise would have been—before Tony.

After the letter dated April 8, which Jeanie received a week after President Roosevelt's death, no letters came for over two weeks. She took refuge in work. Once more, as she had done two springs earlier, she washed the painted ceilings, and this time she papered the front-room walls. Because it was an attic apartment, only the ends of the room were full-ceiling height, so the task was easy. But it did take time. Several nights she worked until after two.

Inspired by Gen, Jeanie tailored a powder-blue wool suit and a short coat of black-and-white houndstooth trimmed with black. But no matter how hard she worked, troubled thoughts haunted her.

May 1, when she finally got a letter from Kenny, written April 21, he didn't even mention President Roosevelt's death.

183

As Long as I Have You

He wrote mainly about how hard they were working and that his company received the Meritorious Service Award. Only three truck companies in the European theater received that award. "We must be doing something OK" he said. He also wrote that they had received an overseas bar for every six months of service. "I'll have a whole armful before I get out of here. I'm only kidding. The war here is as good as over.

"I sure do enjoy our radio. We've still got it even though we keep moving. Tonight I heard my song again—I'll Get By as Long as I Have You.

The war here is as good as over. Those words gave Jeanie the lift she so badly needed. For the first time in weeks she went to bed feeling happy. Kenny would soon be home, the past would be forgotten. They could start living.

Nineteen

If anything gave assurance that the war in Europe was almost over, it was Adolf Hitler's suicide. April 30 headlines screamed the news. Then on May 4, Berchtesgäden, the Führer's mountain fortress, was taken by US troops.

Jeanie caught her breath when she read, the same day, that the Department of War had announced that as soon as Germany surrendered, two million troops would be discharged from the army and six million would be sent to fight in the Pacific.

What would happen to Kenny? Would he be discharged, or sent to the Pacific?

Monday, May 7, news spread at work; Germany had surrendered!

Machines were abandoned, people hugged each other. They all left work early.

As she did on the day the president's death was announced, Jeanie stood out on the high, old porch, tears streaming down her cheeks.

Later, she read the newspaper account of the surrender. General Alfred Jodl signed the unconditional surrender at General Eisenhower's headquarters at Reims.

On the radio, Charles Collingwood of CBS described the ceremony at Reims and added, "The Mad Dog of Europe was put out of the way; the strange, insane monstrosity that was Nazi Germany has been beaten into submission."

May 10, news came that a point system had been established for discharging troops, based on length of service, combat record, and parenthood.

How many points would Kenny have?

But the jubilant mood Jeanie witnessed on the streetcar and on the sidewalks, didn't last long. Again people wore worried frowns as they read about the war in the Pacific.

The war certainly was not over for Gen and her husband stationed in the Philippines. When a letter came with "Dearest Gen" at the top, his name at the bottom and the body of the letter cut out like a window, Gen knew something significant had happened.

Later, when he sent his watch home to be repaired, the jeweler said it had been in salt water. Gen told Jeanie, "I'm sure he was shot down," but she took his letter as evidence that he was now all right.

Day after day, Jeanie waited for some word of where Kenny would be sent, and it was good to be able to share her concern with Thelma several times a week. Early in June, she learned that Thelma was expecting another baby about the end of the year.

CHAPTER NINETEEN

Later, when she thought about the new baby coming, Jeanie wondered if Charles and Thelma would want to take over the rooms upstairs. They certainly could use the additional space. Fear gripped her. Where would she find another apartment? She had not seen a single apartment for rent advertised in the newspapers.

She worried about it for several days before she asked them if they planned to take over the upstairs. They assured her they did not. Charles said that being a bit crowded was a small sacrifice when housing was at such a premium. Jeanie breathed a sigh of relief.

"I can't believe it's been over a year since I went to visit Myrtle and Harry and Grace and Harold in Seneca," Jeanie remarked to Thelma over a cup of tea one evening.

"Now, help me get this straight," Thelma said. "Myrtle and Harold are brother and sister, Harold's wife's name is Grace, and he also has a sister named Grace, is that right?"

Jeanie chuckled. "That's right. It certainly complicates things when a man marries a girl with the same name as his sister."

It was Thelma's turn to chuckle. "Talk about complicated! I'll never get that family of yours straight."

Jeanie nodded. "I just heard that Harold was drafted, and Grace is going to live in a little house near her parents. She's due to have their second baby in June. How could they draft him right now?" Jeanie sighed.

"Remember," she continued, "I told you about Grace's family, the Blombergs? They never minded how many young people were around. We used to get together and play baseball or volleyball in the summer and toboggan and skate in the winter."

187

As Long as I Have You

"I'm glad she can be near her parents," Thelma said, and Jeanie agreed.

Her next letter from Kenny was written the day after VE-day, the end of the war in Europe. "There isn't too much celebration here," he wrote. "We know we can't relax until it's over in the Pacific.

"I know we'll be busy for a while because everyone wants trucks for something. The infantry will be sent home first, so Ray should be home soon. They deserve it. I don't know what's going to happen here yet, but you can bet I'll come home to you as fast as I can."

He added that he needed eighty-five points for discharge but had only sixty-two. "We'll just have to sweat it out together."

The next letter was from Liege, Belgium.

> Now I can write and tell you where I've been. (Seems funny to lick an envelope again. I haven't sealed one for over a year and a half, because the company commander had to censor them.) When we were in Germany, we were stationed near Muenster for quite a while. I drove more runs to the Rhine than I can count. Once we had Germans on three sides of us there. We followed the Ninth Army. It took twenty days to get a two-way bridge across the Rhine. When we first went across, we had to use a pontoon bridge.
>
> I did some driving way down in Bavaria, too. Man! You should see those mountains. Words can't do them justice.
>
> The way it looks, I'll be going to the Pacific. I'm attached to the 91st Air Depot Group now. It's a bomber outfit and a young group. All the men coming in to that outfit have points like myself—in the sixties. But who knows? Just hang in there.

Chapter Nineteen

Jeanie folded the letter and put it under her pillow where she always kept his most recent letters. But she didn't want to reread the part about him going to the Pacific. *Oh, if only the war there would end too!*

June 26, Jeanie tore open a letter from Helen. They seldom wrote to each other because Gram passed Jeanie's letters around, and Helen knew Gram wrote every week. As she read, the tears began to flow. She was still crying when she ran downstairs to tell Thelma what had happened.

Mr. Blomberg, Grace's father, had been killed when his tractor tipped over. Grace and Harold's second baby, Billy, was born just the day before. Harold was in boot camp and couldn't be there. Poor Grace! Poor Mrs. Blomberg! There were several young children still at home.

It helped to be able to share her grief with Thelma.

Now that the war in Europe had ended, Kate was one happy mother. She had plans galore for when Larry came home. "I suppose I'd better not plan too much," she said, flashing her gold-toothed smile. "Guys his age have their own ideas."

Jeanie agreed.

Just when Jeanie had steeled herself for the possibility of Kenny's going to the Pacific, he wrote that he had been transferred to another truck company and had no idea what

189

would happen. He even had to part with "My Baby Jeanie," his faithful truck.

"I left her with your name painted on her. I'd never paint over that. I sure hated to part with her. We sure put on the miles together. I don't have another truck yet. As I said, I don't know what's going on, and I wonder if anyone else does either.

"My buddy Miller is still with me. Sure hated to part with Cannon. Larry Miller and I have been together ever since Mississippi, although we didn't know each other until we got to Fort Warren."

In his next few letters, Kenny wrote that they were "just lying around," but he was glad that he was given five more points for a battle star. "I have to get my mind off of you and how much I want to hold you in my arms, or you'll have a batty husband. I wish they'd give us something to do or send us home. This lying around is driving me nuts."

In his letter dated June 7, he said he was told they would be in Europe until August. Jeanie let out a wail. "August!" And then it would probably take another month to get home—if he would be sent home.

Although Tony had been out of her life almost two months, each time she read Kenny's beautiful assurances of his love and faithfulness, guilt pangs stabbed her. Seeing Tony each morning had been the high point of her day, and there was still an emptiness she couldn't deny.

One noon, after guilt-ridden thoughts had plagued her all morning, Jeanie and Kate took pieces of cardboard out to the fire-escape stairs and sat on them while they ate. They talked about how they were working on a different type of nylon yarn, wondering what it would be used for. But Jeanie's mind was not on nylon yarn. Before they fin-

CHAPTER NINETEEN

ished eating, she asked Kate, "Do you think it's possible to be in love with two men at the same time?"

"Oh no!" Kate groaned. "Not you!"

Jeanie hung her head. How could such an innocent question have given her away?

Kate folded her lunch bag to reuse the next day. "Want to talk about it?" she said kindly.

For a moment the risk seemed too great. What if Kate wanted nothing to do with her? How could she survive solitary lunch periods and a cold shoulder? But the need to tell someone was greater.

Hesitantly, Jeanie tried to describe the intensity of her attraction to Tony—their morning conversations, his caring attitude, even some of her fantasies. At no time did her eyes meet Kate's.

She was about to tell Kate that Tony was gone—out of the picture for good—when Kate grasped her hand.

"Oh, Jeanie! You sound like you think this never happened to anyone before. Look around you! I'm sure you know people who. . . ."

"But not me! Not me!" Jeanie sobbed into her hands. "I love Kenny! How could I want another man?"

Kate took a deep breath. "The way I see it, Jeanie, is that nature is bent on getting male and female together, and it doesn't care one bit if the circumstances aren't right. The attraction is simply there."

"But it's sin!" Jeanie protested.

"Yes," Kate agreed. "And what do you do with sin? We Catholics confess it to a priest and receive absolution. What do you Protestants do?"

Jeanie dabbed her eyes. "I know Jesus died for my sins. I know God forgives."

"Well then? . . ."

Jeanie watched as a breeze caught the waxed paper from her sandwich and carried it down to the alley to join other debris. "There's so much I don't understand."

"Is there someone you could talk with about it?"

Jeanie shook her head. "Not really." She was not willing to confide in those who might be able to help.

"Oh, Jeanie, believe me, I understand what happened."

Jeanie was surprised to see tears in her coworker's eyes—tears of anger.

"It's such a delusion!" Kate said vehemently. "You're sure it's right because you're so happy and you really care about him." She dropped her eyes. "And the attraction is so powerful you can't resist it."

Jeanie blinked in surprise. *Kate really did understand! Of course! Didn't she tell me she was divorced years ago?*

"It's such a lie!" Kate continued, an angry sob breaking her voice. "And, by the time a person sees through it, it's too late!" She caught her breath. "Oh, Jeanie! Get out of it now—before it's too late for you, too!"

Haltingly, Jeanie told her Tony was gone—out of her life forever.

Kate collapsed against the fire escape railing. "Thank God! You and Kenny have such a wonderful love." She put her arm around Jeanie's shoulder. "You'll work this guilt out with God's help, and you'll go on."

They were both silent a moment.

"I envy you," Kate said wistfully "If only I could have seen the truth before it was too late. If only some unforeseen circumstance could have torn us apart before. . . ."

"I'm so sorry Kate."

CHAPTER NINETEEN

Kate fished a handkerchief out of her apron pocket and blew her nose. "It's okay. It was a long time ago. I'm all right now."

That afternoon, as Jeanie changed spools, she wondered why Kate wasn't spared. She had the distinct feeling of being protected. But why her? Why not Kate?

The questions persisted as she worked, and then suddenly she had the answer: *Perhaps no one had prayed for Kate.*

Jeanie caught her breath. *Gram! Gram had prayed.* Gram always prayed for her. *But she didn't even know what was happening.*

The knowledge that she was protected enveloped her like a comforting blanket. She still didn't understand. Maybe someday she would, but right now she was overwhelmed with gratitude. *O God! Thank You.*

That night she didn't dread opening Kenny's letter.

"I sure got a kick out of the Father's Day card," he wrote on June 11. "Wish we didn't have to make Kent and Joannie wait so long.

Jeanie smiled, glad she'd thought of sending it when she had been buying one for his father.

When no letters came for a week, she hoped it meant Kenny was out on a run. It would be better for him than lying around camp.

When a letter finally came, July 3, he said he had been on a short trip and then a long one down around Munich. He had hauled, of all things, dogs. K-9 dogs—watchdogs.

"We traveled the superhighway about all the way. They sure have nice roads. We took a picture of some German planes by the highway. They had used it for a landing strip. That's pretty smart."

193

If Kenny was going to come home in August or September, Jeanie thought, it would be foolish to take her vacation in July as she had planned. Although she was eager to leave those hot machines and the hot apartment, she was just as eager to have their savings account bigger before he got home.

She made up her mind to postpone her July trip "up home" when Kenny's letter of June 27 arrived.

> Well, I have more definite news, but I don't like it. The 91st is going to the States in August, but they're not taking this truck company along. Our officers tell us we're going home in October. We're being held as a reserve here instead of going to the Pacific. So, if everything stays as it is now, we may stay in the States for quite a while after we get back. But you know as well as I do how fast things change. We're turning in all our excess equipment so it can be sent to the Pacific.

Thank God! Kenny is not going to the Pacific. Still, she was disappointed that he would not come home until October. It was somewhat comforting, though, to know she would, after all, be going home in July.

As always, it was good to be home. Surprise! It was obvious that Helen was having another baby.

That week Jeanie and Gram visited the uncles and aunts in the neighborhood and found many changes in the households. At Aunt Ella's house, Myrtle's three little ones kept things lively, but with so many of the children gone it

Chapter Nineteen

was unusually quiet at Uncle George and Aunt Sadie's house. When they left there, Gram said. "I don't think George looks a bit well. Did you see how blue his lips are?"

Jeanie had noticed. She was well aware that a heart defect had partially disabled him for years. He seemed pleased when she told him how often she used the wooden spoons he had carved out of basswood.

Although no one in the family was ever lavish with praise, their warm welcomes gave Jeanie the affirmation she needed. Now and then someone remarked how she has been such a good wife throughout the war. But, as welcome as those compliments were, they only made her feel more guilty.

One afternoon, she walked alone by the river, guilt weighing down her every step. She had lost count of the many times she had confessed her sin to God, feeling she accepted His forgiveness, only to have that guilt come flooding over her again.

> I think it's all dealt with, and back it comes again. It's like when Gram and I used to hoe our little garden after a rain, foot by foot until there wasn't a weed to be seen—just clean rows of beets, carrots, peas, and nice, dark red Wisconsin soil. But two days later, I'd look out there and could hardly see the ground for chickweed and quack grass. Is this the way it's going to be the rest of my life?

Fortunately, there were others to think about, and Jeanie had little time to dwell on her guilt while she was back home in Wisconsin. Though the war in Europe was over, and everyone was sure the one in the Pacific would also soon end, it wasn't easy trying to cheer Kenny's mother. She expected Ray home any time but was afraid he would have a difficult time adjusting to civilian life. And though she was eager for Kenny to get home, she was not optimistic because she heard that quartermaster units would be the last ones released.

She would have been even more depressed if she had read the letter from Kenny that was waiting for Jeanie when she got back to Chicago. He said that there was talk again that they were slated to go directly to the Pacific instead of getting a furlough.

"Maybe that is best. I just don't know how I'm going to be able to leave you again. It's been over two years since we've been together. My life is miserable without you."

Once more Jeanie's life was like that dark, starless night. Where could she find the courage to go on?

In his next letter, Kenny was in a lighter mood. "Guess what! I saw My Baby Jeanie today—the first one that is. I've named every truck I've had My Baby Jeanie. A guy from our old company was driving her. She's got over forty-thousand miles on her and is still going strong. That's a lot of miles for this kind of driving. Gee, I could hardly believe my eyes. Funny how a guy can get attached to a piece of machinery."

Saturday, August 4, Jeanie felt so weak she stayed in bed most of the day. No matter how hard she breathed she couldn't get enough air. When she went down to get the mail she was barely able to climb back up all those stairs. Instead of feeling sadness, loneliness, or even guilt, it was as if her emotions were drained out of her.

Lying on her bed, she tore open Kenny's letter. "Baby! That talk about us going directly to the Pacific was just a rumor. Our lieutenant told us today that our orders are to come directly to the States."

CHAPTER NINETEEN

Tears of relief—but also of fatigue—slid down Jeanie's cheeks. But October seemed such a long way off. More likely, it would be November before he actually got home. She tried to think of things to do in the house, of ideas for new clothes, but her mind was blank. All she wanted to do was to sleep, and when she did, it was a restless, dream-plagued sleep.

Monday, August 6, Jeanie dragged herself to work. If only it weren't so hot.

Late in the afternoon, Joe, a mechanic, ran from one worker to the next, spreading the news that a US bomber dropped such a powerful bomb on Hiroshima, Japan, that it wiped out the whole city. It was called an "atomic bomb". "They've gotta quit now," he added jubilantly.

It was easier for Jeanie to get up the stairs that night. She listened to newscast after newscast, trying to imagine a bomb that could level four square miles of buildings. It was said to have the power equal to twenty-thousand tons of TNT. *Surely those poor people died instantly.*

The official communiqué from the White House was repeated throughout the evening. A brief description of what had happened concluded with:

> It was to spare the Japanese people from utter destruction that the ultimatum of July 26 was issued at Potsdam. Their leaders promptly rejected that ultimatum. If they do not now accept our terms, they may expect a rain of ruin from the air, the likes of which has never been seen.

Surely, Jeanie thought, there would be immediate surrender.

The nation held its breath. One day. Two days. Still no word of surrender.

197

As Long as I Have You

The third day the world was shocked again when a second atomic bomb was dropped on Nagasaki. The following day, the Japanese cabinet sent a message through Switzerland, accepting the terms of the Potsdam ultimatum. Except for the actual signing of surrender terms, the war was over.

August 14, Emperor Hirohito announced defeat to his people, and the city of Chicago went wild.

That evening, Lenore ran up Jeanie's stairs shouting, "Let's go celebrate!"

She said her father was waiting downstairs to escort them on the el to join the celebration downtown in the Loop.

People still appeared a bit dazed on the el, but down on State Street thousands of cheering people swarmed up and down the street as every whistle, horn, and bell loudly proclaimed victory. Sailors hugged and kissed every girl within reach. Lenore's father made a valiant effort to ward them off.

"It's over! It's over! It's over!" Jeanie sobbed into her pillow that night. Now all the troops could come home.

Twenty

The image of that horrible atom-bomb mushroom diluted the joy Emma felt over the end of the war with Japan. What monstrous weapon had man created? If they could make one that would wipe out four square miles, what would keep them from making one that would wipe out forty—or four hundred?

Was it cowardly to be glad that she wouldn't be around to see what would happen in another twenty years? Over and over she thought, *What would Papa say?* Anytime there was an astounding, new event, she longed to share it with him and to know what insights he would have into the situation. Al's views on life were still very much a part of her.

Oh, but she was happy that the boys would be coming home. Not one of her grandsons had been killed or even badly injured. Now she must pray, not only for their safe return, but for their adjustment to civilian life. *Where,* she wondered, *will they all find jobs? They'll get married and* want to start their own homes. Are there enough apartments and houses?

"Blessed assurance,/Jesus is mine," she sang as she walked about the yard, picking up twigs and bits of paper as she always did. A breeze brushed her face, and she looked up at the swaying pine trees. She stood very still, trying to recall that wonderful sound, then shook her head when memory failed her, and walked on. In spite of all the turmoil in the world, her own little corner of it was peaceful.

She dumped the contents of her apron in the wood box, walked back out to the porch swing, and swinging gently, finished her song.

> Perfect submission./All is at rest./I in my Savior am happy and blest./Watching and waiting,/looking above,/ Filled with His goodness,/lost in His love.

Oh, if only the whole world could know His peace right in the midst of trouble. If only Jeanie knew that peace. Emma sighed. *Someday Jeanie will come to know it—someday.*

In his letter dated August 6, Kenny didn't even mention the atomic bomb. He had been on the road for several days. "We started out with a convoy of twenty-four trucks, and they split us up over and over until here I am in Germany, about sixty miles from Munich, and there are only four of us left. Miller and I are still together, but we had to pull a few strings to work that out.

CHAPTER TWENTY

Even in his letter written August 11, Kenny didn't mention the atomic bomb or that the war was over in Japan until the third page. He wrote,

> Some fellows around here are saying that Japan has accepted our peace terms. I hope so, but I don't believe it yet until I read about it. But even if they didn't, with this new bomb, it won't be long now before they will. I suppose everyone's celebrating back there, but I just can't see any sense in celebrating until I'm home with you, Baby. I'm very thankful that the war is about over, but I'll leave the celebrating until our day!

Jeanie was surprised. She thought the guys over there would be simply wild with joy.

When she mentioned this to Kate at work, Kate said, "I guess it's not easy to realize it's over as long as you're still living in barracks and working every day as usual."

> Well, our orders were canceled again, [Kenny wrote August 23]. I found out the other day that the orders to come home, instead of going to the Pacific, had been canceled before, only we didn't know about it. We were scheduled to be shipped directly to the Pacific September 20! The war didn't end a day too soon. Now the second orders have been canceled. We are supposed to go to the staging area in November. Just think, if the war hadn't ended, I would have been on my way over there in a couple more weeks. I know there's still plenty of work to do to get rid of materials the Germans could use to make more weapons. Until that's done, some of us will stay here. I tell you, Baby, it would take the biggest wrecker this army has to pull me away from you when I get home. I'm never going to leave you again.

201

That evening Jeanie told Thelma, "I should have learned by now not to get my hopes up about any special date." She sighed. "Sometimes I wish I could turn my thoughts off like a light switch."

Thelma nodded. "I think I know how you feel, but remember that every day brings Kenny closer to home, no matter when that is."

Even though their Red Cross bandage work ended, Gen and Jeanie still got together quite often. One evening, as they were taking a walk, Gen said, "Well, now that the letters aren't censored anymore, Warren was able to tell me what really happened back in May. They were shot down last spring!"

"Oh my goodness! Just like you thought."

"He said there were eleven men in all, several were killed, some wounded. They had been floating in life rafts about a day and a half when they heard a baby crying. It was dark and they were afraid it could be a Japanese trick, so they stayed quiet. But it really was a baby, and some Chinese people picked them up and took them to the mainland. From there they got back to their base in Luzon."

"That gives me goose bumps!" Jeanie told her.

"One more day," Gen continued, "and they would have been reported missing in action."

She hugged Gen. "Now I really have goose bumps."

"Oh, I know. Talk about grateful. Warren thinks he'll be home about November but probably not discharged for a while."

Kate's son, Larry, came home and, as she anticipated, was out and gone much of the time. "He can't decide if he wants to go to school under the GI bill or try to find a job."

CHAPTER TWENTY

"Sounds like a great opportunity to go to school," said Jeanie.

Kate nodded. "But you know these young people. They have to make up their own minds." She looked at Jeanie as if suddenly remembering that Jeanie was one of those young people. "Sometimes I forget how young you are. You are exceptionally mature for your age, you know."

Sunday evening Jeanie had just come home from Vi's when Thelma called her to the phone. "You have a long-distance call from Wisconsin."

Jeanie's heart leaped into in her throat. No one made long-distance calls unless it was an emergency. Had something happened to Gram?

The connection was so bad she could hardly hear Roy's voice. "George died today," he told her. "The funeral will be Wednesday. Can you get in touch with Hank?"

"I'll try," she promised him.

She choked back tears as she told Thelma. "Uncle George had a bad heart, and the last time I saw him, he looked terribly pale. But poor Aunt Sadie! It's a big family, just like the Blomberg's, and there are several young children still at home. "Jeanie shook her head. "Mr. Blomberg's name was George, too, and he was a father of a big family. . . . Two of them so close together."

Thelma expressed her sympathy. "You'll be going home?"

Jeanie groaned. "Yes, but I have to let my uncle Hank know. I've visited them a few times. They live a few blocks south of Madison street near the stadium. I'd better get down there before it gets dark. It's not a good neighborhood."

Thelma frowned. "Charles should be home in an hour or two. Do you want to wait and have him go with you?"

203

Jeanie declined, and still wearing her bright red suit, she ran to the el.

When she knocked on the door of the apartment where she had previously visited them, a black lady came to the door. She had no idea where Hank and his family now lived.

Jeanie stood on the littered sidewalk, searching her memory for some clue. She knew Hank frequented the bars along Madison Street, and once she had heard him talk about The Billy Goat.

It took all the courage she could muster to go into that bar alone. Although Hank wasn't there, the bartender knew who he was. But he had no idea where he lived.

A group of men at the bar suggested another bar a few blocks away, and before she turned to leave they made comments about her figure, which left her face as red as her suit.

The scene was repeated at the next bar and the next. But at the third one, an old man told her he knew where Hank's mother-in-law lived—a block south in the house right next to the el.

As Jeanie hurried along, staggering men leered in her face, but thank God none of them touched her. She turned her head when she saw a row of them facing a wall. She could hear what they were doing, and she hurried on.

She found the house and after a deep breath and a brief prayer she knocked on the door. It was the right house, but his mother-in-law had no idea where Hank was. She promised to give him the message about his brother George when she saw him.

Jeanie lost no time getting back on the el.

It was nearly ten when Thelma again called Jeanie to the phone. It was Hank.

CHAPTER TWENTY

"What brother died?" he demanded. He had been told only that one of his brothers had died.

Before they hung up, he and Jeanie agreed that Tuesday they would meet at gate 15 in Union Station and take the train up to Tomahawk.

Monday, when Jeanie told her boss where she had been the night before, he scolded her for going alone and added, "Your guardian angel must have been with you!"

Tuesday, Jeanie dragged her luggage to gate 15. No Hank. She waited and waited, not boarding until the very last moment. *I might have known,* she thought.

As always, she had to struggle through all the heavy doors and through car after car to the head of the train. When she finally reached the Tomahawk car, there was Hank sitting comfortably as could be. He flashed his charming smile and said, "I knew you'd find me. I got tired of standing there. Got a bad leg again."

Hank always had a bad leg, or two. He had trouble with varicose veins, and his constant drinking did them no good.

On the ride up to Tomahawk, Jeanie's emotions ranged from wanting to hug him to wanting to shake him. Hank was fourteen when she was born, and Gram had taken her to live with her and her three young sons, so he was more like her big brother than an uncle. She thought of the teasing and laughter, but she also remembered the agonizing nights when she'd wake up to see Gram pacing the floor, waiting for him to come home from a dance. She loved to hear him tell hunting stories to a neighbor man, who often stopped to visit. How proud she had been when he had pitched for the Rib Lake baseball team. Those were his glory days, before drinking stole his ability.

205

As Long as I Have You

But in spite of her concern and dismay, it was good to be with Hank. Jeanie loved to hear him tell stories of what he observed in the animal world. "Remember the time you came home from the woods and asked me to get your canteen out of your backpack so Gram would wash it, and when I unbuckled the strap, the paw of a wildcat's cub you had trapped popped out at me?"

That triggered a long series of animal stories that Jeanie had heard before but didn't mind hearing again. *What might Hank have been,* she wondered, *if he had gotten an education—and could have conquered his drinking habit?*

When they arrived, Jeanie found Gram was taking her son's death surprisingly well. "Poor boy!" Gram sighed as they stood by the casket. "He has suffered so long. My, he was a handsome man, and only fifty-four."

At the funeral, Aunt Sadie sat surrounded by her children: Dorothy, Norma, Glen, Ardis, Owen, Betty, George Jr., Bunetta, Gardia, Lora, and Jack.

Jeanie thought of the time they all had been taken ill with scarlet fever and were quarantined for weeks. She had gone with other children from school, had peeked through the windows and had left papers and books that could be burned. Books had to be burned before the quarantine could be lifted, because it was believed that scarlet fever germs could live for years between the pages of a book.

She remembered Dorothy's wedding, when aunts, uncles, and cousins swarmed all over the house and yard. What a happy day that had been.

At the cemetery, Jeanie realized that at this very moment three years ago, she had been putting on her own wedding dress. She found herself unable to stop crying for

206

Chapter Twenty

several moments. But only she knew that not all of her tears were for Uncle George.

Only one letter from Kenny was waiting when Jeanie got home. He had some significant news. Early in October they would be sent back to Belgium, then the whole company would go to battalion headquarters to turn in their equipment.

"After that's over," he wrote, "I don't know if the high-point men will go first or if the whole company will be sent home together. It sure is a complicated process.

"If it wasn't for this ocean between us, I'd start walking to get back to the best wife in the world!"

That phrase never failed to give Jeanie a pang of guilt.

September 16 he wrote that he and others had been sent to a small castle near Munich to pick up books and documents from a chemical factory. They picked up seven truckloads in all.

> How would you like to read all those books, Baby? I was told they were written in four different languages. We're trying to get our trucks ready to turn in, but everybody's still yelling for trucks, so we have to keep working. Now we heard we should be ready to turn in our equipment within thirty days.
>
> Just ten more days and we'll be married three years. Sometimes I feel so robbed! Think of all that time we could have been together! But we'll make up for it, won't we Baby? You're all I ever want. You're the best wife any man could have.

That night when Jeanie baby-sat with Elizabeth, guilt again wrapped her in a depressing fog. Somehow she had to get out of this mood before she tried to write to Kenny.

She looked around for something to read, but all she could find was Thelma and Charles's Bible. Sometimes the Bible would be on the kitchen table, sometimes on the dining room table, sometimes here beside the sofa. *They must really read it,* Jeanie thought.

She leaned her head back against the sofa and closed her eyes. No pastor ever told her not to read the Bible, but she somehow accepted the idea that only someone with seminary training could understand it—that it didn't do much good to read the Bible by yourself.

She smiled as she remembered going to the Baptist church in Ogema with her cousins Amy and Rose. Bible reading was definitely encouraged there. Once, after hearing someone speak about reading the whole Bible through in a year, the three of them determined to do just that. She never knew how far Amy and Rose got, but she was only into the book of Numbers when she gave up.

Gram didn't often read the Bible either. When she did, she'd stand by the light of the east window, her lips moving as she read. Once she remarked about all the good things in Proverbs and suggested that Jeanie should read them too.

Jeanie knew some of what was in the Bible, because she heard portions of the Gospels and the Epistles each Sunday at church. But it never occurred to her to read the Bible for help in living her life. Now she needed some help with this plaguing guilt.

She reached for the big, leather book, flipped it open, and began to page through it. It had notes written in it and

CHAPTER TWENTY

some spots were underlined. She never heard of anyone writing in any book, much less the Holy Bible.

In Luke, she found the wonderful, familiar story of Jesus' birth. And then the parable of the lost sheep and the parable of the prodigal son. She also found the story of the unjust steward. It was like meeting old friends. John 3:16 was underlined. That was familiar, too, because she memorized the verse years ago, early in her teens, when the young people had met with the pastor those Saturday mornings.

She skimmed through one underlined section to another until she reached Romans 8:28. She'd heard Gram quote that one, about all things working together for good to them that loved God and were called according to His purpose. She wanted to love God, but how could you love someone so far away? Was she "called according to His purpose?" She wasn't at all sure of that. And yet, there was something deep in her heart—a sort of knowing—that God was concerned with her.

O God, she prayed, *I do want to love you. I want to be close to you.*

Now she found in Philippians chapter 4 the verse the pastor at the big church used for the text of his sermon on worry. "Be careful for nothing; but in every thing by prayer and supplication with thanksgiving let your requests be made known unto God." Oh, how she wanted to keep from worrying!

On and on she went, thumbing through Thelma and Charles's Bible. She realize how many verses she had memorized. Then she read an underlined one she had not memorized: 1 John 1:9. "If we confess our sins, he is faithful and just to forgive us our sins, and to cleanse us from all unrighteousness."

She read it over and over, and each time it was as if her fog of guilt lifted a little bit more. "He is faithful!" she whispered. "He will forgive me and cleanse me from this sin!"

When Thelma came home, Jeanie fairly floated upstairs.

That night she was able to truly pray. And, as she felt sleep stealing her consciousness, it was like loving arms holding her close.

Twenty-one

When Jeanie heard the crunch of dry leaves under her feet as she walked toward Vi's one October evening, she felt the same wave of apprehension as she had last autumn. She dreaded the dark fall days and the bleak winter winds. But this winter, she reminded herself, would be different. Kenny would surely be home soon, and it wouldn't matter how early the sun set or how cold the wind blew once they were back in each other's arms.

Jeanie put a smile on her face when she greeted Vi, but Vi did not return her smile. Instead she blinked back angry tears as she explained that the landlady had ordered them to move. "Where in the world are we supposed to find anyone who will rent to a couple with four children in this day and age?" She picked up little Bobby and set her coffee cup out of his reach.

Jeanie knew Art and Vi's landlady had been complaining about their children running and jumping—that she couldn't

As Long as I Have You

take all that noise above her—but now she really meant business. They would have to move as soon as possible.

Vi shifted Bobby on her lap and said, "We've tracked down every ad we've seen, but no one will rent to us because of the children."

Jeanie didn't know what to say. What a spot to be in. Art's mother was with them too, so they'd need an extra bedroom.

"We've even thought of trying to buy a house on contract, but all we have is a couple hundred dollars we've been saving for a car." Vi sighed. "I suppose we could borrow some on our insurance policies."

"We could probably lend you some," said Jeanie, "but I'd have to talk it over with Kenny." She changed the subject. "You are so cute!" she told little Bobby. His hair stood straight up, as if he had a crew cut. "Just think, he's almost two years old, and Kenny hasn't even seen him!"

Vi took a sip of her coffee. "Any idea when he'll be home? I know it's different every time I talk with you."

Jeanie pulled little Billy up on her lap and gave him a cracker. "All I know is they're getting ready to turn in their equipment at battalion headquarters." She chuckled. "He's getting pretty feisty these days. He said when that equipment is turned in, he's done working and they'd better not ask him to drive another truck."

Vi chuckled. "Oh, he won't put up with any nonsense, and I can't blame him. It's been a long wait. It must have been hard to see so many guys go home ahead of him."

Jeanie nodded. "I know, but he says he got off easy during the war, so now he has to make up for it. He wouldn't want to be in the infantry." Jeanie sighed. "It's so good to know Ray is back in the States, even though he doesn't have his discharge yet. I wonder what he'll do when he gets out."

212

CHAPTER TWENTY-ONE

"He told me he wants to take a little vacation before he goes back to work at Garcey Lighting Company. After what he has been through, I can hardly blame him."

The few letters that came from Kenny during the first part of October were full of frustration and uncertainty. Then, in his letter of October 12, he said, "We're all done working! We've turned in all our equipment. Don't know when we'll leave for the staging area, but it can't be too soon."

There were no more letters that week—or the next.

It was difficult for Jeanie to keep writing letters, wondering if Kenny was going to get them. The second of November, those letters started to come back, and she knew there was no point in writing anymore.

But her habit of writing to Kenny each night for nearly three years was not easily broken. When evening came, she found herself pacing the length of the apartment. There were others she could write to, but what was she to tell them? She tried to read, but found that her eyes would glide down a whole page, and at the end of it she didn't know a thing she had read.

It didn't matter now if the streetcar didn't get through the green lights on the way home from work. What point was there in going home? When she saw white spots in the mailbox she no longer ran across the street.

Of course, she welcomed letters from others.

Helen wrote that Ruby was discharged from the WACS in September, the same time Chet was discharged. "Well," Helen continued, "it's quite a story. You'll have to hear them tell it sometime. Ruby hadn't had enough points to be discharged in September when Chet had gotten home. On top of that, she'd had orders to go overseas. So she had to choose between staying in service and going over-

213

seas, or being bold and telling Chet they needed to get married right away so she'd have enough points to get out as the wife of a veteran. They hadn't seen each other for three-and-half years, you know.

"Well, she got up courage enough to tell Chet, and they were married—just like that! That night, one had to go back to Fort Sheridan the other to Camp Grant. I don't remember who went where."

Jeanie could just see Ruby's flushed face, knowing how easily she blushed when she had to be so bold.

Day after day—even hour after hour—Jeanie tried to determine when Kenny would be home. If he had gone to the staging area soon after his last letter and if he'd left right away, he could be home any day.

There was little in the apartment that Jeanie did not clean that first week in November. She also hauled out Kenny's clothes, which had been packed away for almost three years, wondering if any of them would still fit. She washed everything that was washable, just in case. It was wonderful to again have his underwear in the dresser drawers. She hoped they would still fit, because it was almost impossible to find any in the stores.

Over the years, cotton items gradually disappeared from the stores. Still, she was shocked when she went into Weiboldts in Oak Park and saw nothing but empty display islands where the towels and sheets used to be. A saleslady told her that a small order of stock would come in and would be gone in an hour. She advised Jeanie to put her name on a list for a dress shirt if her husband needed one when he came home.

Jeanie did, ordering one size larger than Kenny used to wear.

Chapter Twenty-One

She hated to leave the house for a moment, except for time at work. She mentally kicked herself for not having given Kenny Thelma and Charles's phone number. But even if she had, knowing Kenny, he would probably just walk in some day without calling. Oh, she hoped she'd be home when he did.

"It could be several weeks yet," Charles warned. "He may have to wait in the staging area for a while."

Jeanie knew he was right, but she didn't want to hear that.

Kenny's mother wrote that just about all the servicemen in Rib Lake were home again—all but Kenny.

"I'm going to take off from work awhile when my husband comes home," Jeanie warned her boss.

There was a lot of work to be done, but her boss just smiled and nodded.

Never had the challenge to make each day count been more difficult for Jeanie. She didn't want to start any new sewing projects; there was only daily housework to do; and she couldn't make plans to go anywhere because she didn't want to be away from home any more than necessary. Whenever she went to Vi's, or any other place, she left the phone number with Thelma.

Kenny and Jeanie taken the day Kenny left after his only furlough—July 1943.

Before she went to bed, she always reread some of Kenny's letters, even though it still hurt to read his precious assurances of faithfulness and his confidence in her. She would take a deep breath and tell herself, *When we confess our sins, he is faithful and just to forgive us our sins, and to cleanse us from all unrighteousness.* It helped. Now when she thought of Tony, it was as if the brief streetcar romance happened to someone else, not to her.

When she couldn't think of anything else to do, she would turn the radio on low, lie down on the bed, and dream of days to come. *Ah, each evening there would be wonderful kisses at the door. His bath run, clean clothes laid out, "mm mm,"* he'd say, *"something smells good! What's for dinner?"* There would be flowers on the table and candles. No, no candles. Kenny hated candlelit dinners. "I want to see what I'm eating," he told her the time she'd tried it. But, maybe if she used several candles. . . .

And there would be the clink of silver on china, the tinkle of ice in crystal goblets . . . well, maybe not crystal for a while.

He would tell her about the people at work—the funny things—and she'd listen. And she'd tell him what she had read and heard and thought that day.

Will he still do ridiculous things, she wondered, *like dump me into the tub with my clothes on or shutting me out on the porch in only my slip?*

What if he changed? Maybe those years in the army have taken all the fun out of him.

What if he imagined me much more attractive than I really am? Will he be shocked when he sees me again? Disappointed?

Over and over he had written, "We're just made for each other." *What if he doesn't feel that way anymore? What if I don't feel that way anymore?*

What if we don't have the same values anymore?

Chapter Twenty-One

She had written dream-filled letters—about buying a car, taking a trip, and buying a house, but now that the war was over and he was coming home, those dreams seemed foolish. They needed to stay right where they were for now and build a solid foundation again. Anyway, there simply weren't any cars for sale, so that canceled any traveling—unless they took a train, and that wouldn't be much fun. "Oh, I'm not going to think all these negative things!" she said out loud. She got up from the bed and paced around the house.

In a few moments she dug out his letters and read over a few and felt more assured that Kenny was still the same. With his sweet words in mind, she stretched out again and imagined that the dishes were done and he was reading the paper. She smiled. She'd creep up under his newspaper like she used to do. He'd kiss her, and then she'd snuggle down with her head on his shoulder and wait for him to finish reading. They'd listen to the radio and laugh together or just talk.

Then it would be dark and quiet . . . and there would be giggles and love sounds, and she wouldn't know where she left off and he began. She hadn't dared even think about that for a long time. Afterward, she would lie with her head on his shoulder—in their *us* world—and they would marvel at their love.

Soon she'd be pregnant. What would it be like to carry a baby? Kent? Joannie? *Mm-m . . . warm little body . . . downy little head. . . .* "I'd better not get so wrapped up in the baby that I forget Kenny!" she warned herself.

But first he had to get home.

About the middle of November, Jeanie began to play the, he's getting off the el, game. She would hear the el train pull into the station and the tramping of feet as people walked along the wooden platform and down the stairs. And she'd imagine: *Now he's getting off the train . . . walking down the platform . . . down the stairs . . . through the station . . . down the street to the corner . . . through the gangway . . . up the first flight . . . across the downstairs porch . . . up the long flight to the landing . . . up the little flight . . . at the door!*

But there never was any knock on the door.

Thanksgiving Day, when Jeanie was having dinner at Vi's, she said, "Wouldn't this be a Thanksgiving Day to remember if Kenny came home today?"

Art and Vi agreed, but said nothing more. What could they say?

Grandma Emma, always knitting.

"I haven't had a letter for a month," she wrote to Gram that evening. She was writing at least two letters a week to Gram while she was waiting for Kenny.

> When Kenny was first gone, you told me time would go faster if I kept busy. You were right. I kept so busy I dropped into bed exhausted every night. But now I'm really having a hard time trying to keep busy.
>
> I'm always listening for footsteps on the stairs and imagining over and over that he's getting off the el and walking down the stairs, across the street, and up our stairs. Sometimes it seems like the day he'll be home is

CHAPTER TWENTY-ONE

moving farther away instead of closer. Oh, Mama, I'm so tired of waiting.

She thought of telling Gram her many fears about Kenny—and their future. It would be good to have Gram write back and assure her those fears were false. No, she decided, she would not burden Gram with them.

The first Monday in December, Jeanie scowled at herself in the mirror and groaned. There was a sore red bump at the right of her nose and another one on her chin. She dabbed powder on them but they still looked red. Not only that, she felt the same monthly cramps that had plagued her since she was twelve.

She got through the afternoon with the help of two aspirin. She huddled in a miserable lump on the streetcars and when she got home she rolled right into bed with a hot water bottle. "Of all nights," she moaned, "this will probably be the one Kenny will come!"

He didn't.

She twisted and turned, again plagued by negative thoughts. She had heard about several men who had come back from the service not seeming to care if they ever got a job. Their excuse was that they needed time to adjust. What if Kenny didn't care? What if the war had affected him so much emotionally that he couldn't hold a steady job?

Still Jeanie's biggest fear was that he would be disappointed when he saw her. That week she started the red negligee routine. Kenny had sent her money for their anniversary, and she had bought a red jersey negligee with frosty white embroidery on the lapels. He loved to see her in red.

Each evening she would take a bath—a hasty one—in case he came to the door while she was in the tub. Then

219

As Long as I Have You

she would put on the red negligee, brush her hair under in a pageboy, sweep the sides up, and pin them in rolls. After that she would carefully put on her makeup, add a dash of the perfume he had sent from Paris, and wait.

At ten, she would take off the negligee, wash off the makeup, roll her hair in curlers, and go to bed.

"I feel silly going through that whole routine every night," she told Kate, "but I want Kenny to always remember how I looked when he first saw me." She sighed. "Oh, I hope he's not disappointed."

"Disappointed in what?"

Jeanie dropped her eyes. "In how I look."

Kate gave her an impatient wave. "Oh, for goodness sakes! He's not going to be disappointed! I didn't know you when he went away, but I can't imagine that you've grown anything but more attractive."

Jeanie smiled her thanks. Still, when she was back at her machines the fears crowded in again.

As another week went by, it seemed that every day a new fear would creep up to taunt her along with the old ones. She tried to fight them off by thinking of all the loving things Kenny had written. Another week began. "I feel like a guitar string being tightened a little more every day," she told Kate.

Kenny's mother wrote, "For goodness sakes, call me when he comes. I can't stand this much longer!"

Twenty-two

Jeanie almost wished she had to work that third Saturday in December. The time would have gone by faster.

She ran to the grocery store and snatched a few items. After that, she cleaned the house—again! She could think of nothing more to do, so she went down and talked with Thelma, keeping a close watch out the kitchen window.

Later she tried to kill some more time by taking a nap but couldn't go to sleep. So she played the el game a few times until she got so nervous she had to get up and pace. He just had to come home soon.

At five she opened a can of tomato soup and made a cheese sandwich. She sat eating on the kitchen stool by the cabinet so she could see out the back-door window. She remembered how she had eaten all her meals there for at least a year before she could bear sitting at the table alone.

Would Kenny be happy in these little rooms after being all over the world? Would he be content to live such a quiet, uneventful life?

After washing the dishes, she took a bath and put on the red negligee. She had one side of her hair pinned up when she heard a knock. She bounded out of the bathroom, one side of her hair hanging down, the other pinned up . . . and there he was!

Laughter, happy tears, fierce kisses . . . the feel of rough woolen khaki, unfamiliar scent . . .

"Let me see you!"

"Oh, my hair!" She tore herself away, snatched a bobby pin and rolled up her hair. Then she was back in his arms.

She felt his tears on her cheek. And then his kisses. And more kisses.

"You're so strong. You're hurting me!"

"I'm sorry." He briefly let her go. "Oh, Baby!" And they were back in the clinch again.

"This is it!" she told herself. "This is the moment you have dreamed of for years!" She knew she should be happy, but she couldn't feel it. It was as though she had somehow forgotten how to feel. Eventually Kenny took off his uniform jacket and looked around as Jeanie pointed out the wallpaper, the little shelves, the new linoleum on the kitchen floor—all the things she had changed in the apartment while he'd been gone.

He murmured approval, but his eyes immediately turned back to her.

"Are you hungry?"

He shrugged. "I don't know. . . . Got any milk?"

She nodded, glad she had gone to the store.

She took the milk out of the refrigerator, then cheese and lunch meat for sandwiches, self-conscious of every move she made, because his eyes never left her.

CHAPTER TWENTY-TWO

"Boy! I wish my buddies could see you—especially Miller and Cannon."

What does he mean? Could she really believe he wasn't disappointed?

"Your mom wrote and asked us to call when you came. It's been rough on your folks, waiting and waiting."

"I'll do that," Kenny said, buttering a slice of bread. "I'm sure glad to know Ray is back in the States. He's the one they had to worry about."

Jeanie watched his every move and expression. The way he gestured with his thumb curved back, that was familiar— and his sudden grin revealing the separation between his front teeth. But the frown line between his heavy brows and the firm set of his jaw had not been there three years ago.

He munched his sandwich and said, "Man! I thought they'd never get us on a ship. We sat around and played cards day after day. Thought I'd go nuts."

He drank the glass of milk without stopping and poured another one.

"What was it like on the troopship?"

He shook his head. "No joyride, I can tell you. All we did was get in line for chow in the morning, stand in line three or four hours, eat, and get back in line again for the next meal. They fed us twice a day. I never want to stand in another line as long as I live!"

Jeanie laughed. "Well, I can't guarantee you won't have to. Life is full of waiting lines, you know."

"I was lucky . . . in a way. I got boils on my neck." He turned so she could see one healed scar and another still an angry red. "I went to the sick bay, and they gave me a note so I could take a shower every day. Were the guys jealous! I told 'em I'd trade a boil for a shower. That shut 'em up."

223

Later, when his rough, woolen uniform was lain aside, he held her close and said huskily, "You're even more beautiful than I remembered."

One fear fell away. "I was so afraid you'd be disappointed," she said against his chest. The mirror didn't tell her she was beautiful, but that didn't matter—just so Kenny thought she was.

During the night, Jeanie awoke, startled to find she was not alone in bed. She crept to the bathroom, thinking this night was almost like their wedding night—except before that night, they were together nearly every day all summer. Now it was as if she went to bed with someone she hardly knew.

She walked softly across the kitchen to the door window where she had spent so many lonely moments. "Lord," she whispered, "I thank you for bringing him safely home, but I'm scared. He's so rough, so loud. I know he doesn't mean to, but he hurts me every time he touches me. Help us through this time of getting used to each other again. Help me understand what he's been through, and make me the kind of wife he needs."

Looking out over the rooftops, Jeanie relived the whole coming-home evening in her mind, hoping that as she did, she would feel what she wanted to feel.

She cringed at all the vulgar words he'd used in the course of conversation, totally unaware of how they shocked her. *Will he always talk like that?* She would just die if he talked like that in front of Charles and Thelma or Lenore and the other girls she knew. She wanted to be proud of him, not feel scared that he would embarrass her.

But even the possibility of being embarrassed didn't bother her as much as not being able to feel what she wanted to feel. Instead of the ecstatic elation she expected, she found

CHAPTER TWENTY-TWO

herself groping for feeling. Was it because she hadn't come to the full realization that Kenny really was home? *What's wrong with me?* The more she tried to feel, the more any feeling eluded her. She sighed, and tiptoed back to bed and lay back down without touching him.

The next morning, Jeanie was still conscious of her every move, because Kenny watched her so closely. "Are you going to wear your uniform over to Art and Vi's?" she asked him as she buttered toast.

He shrugged. "Can't wait to get out of the danged thing, but I don't know if any of my old clothes will fit me."

Most of them didn't. He had to pull in his stomach to button any of his trousers and he could barely button the one shirt that could be worn with a tie. "You mean I have to wear this to church tomorrow?" he asked, quickly opening the top button.

Jeanie shrugged. "I guess so, unless you want to wear your uniform."

Kenny scowled. "How come you didn't buy me a bigger shirt? You shoulda known I'd be bigger."

"I put our name on a list for one." She hung up the shirt he had tossed on the rocker. "But I have no idea how soon it will come."

He looked puzzled. "You mean a guy can't go out and buy a shirt?"

Jeanie shook her head. "Not a dress shirt."

Kenny sat down on the edge of the bed to try on his dress shoes. "You know, I never thought of people back here not being able to get everything they want."

Jeanie gave a wry laugh. "You should go out and try to buy towels or sheets." She told him about the bare store counters.

225

As Long as I Have You

Fortunately, his shoes still fit.

Jeanie took her underwear out of the drawer to take to the bathroom. She was not about to dress in front of him yet. "You know, I think it would be good if you wore your uniform over to Vi's. That way, the children would remember Uncle Kenny coming home as a soldier."

"I suppose so," he said, pulling on his old, gold sweater. "At least this still fits."

"What does that sweater remind you of?" she asked him.

He met her eyes. "The car accident."

Jeanie nodded. "People still say it's a miracle some of us weren't killed."

They were both quiet a moment, remembering that September night four years ago when Kenny was driving in the rain and the car, with six young people in it, had rolled over on a curve.

Kenny reached for her hand. "I hope I never have to live through another time like that. There you were, your hair stuck in the car door, and we couldn't get you out, and there was Curley bleeding all over the place, and we were trying to stop a car to take her to the doctor. I'd still like to find that first son-of-a-gun who stopped and wouldn't take her when he saw how she was bleeding."

"Ouch!" Jeanie cried when Kenny squeezed her hand. She pulled it away and quietly said, "But Ray Becker did stop and took Pete and Curley to the doctor."

He took her hand again, this time holding it gently. "And we did get you out when more people came to lift the car."

"I'd better get dressed." She went into the bathroom thinking it was good to talk about something they had both experienced—even a painful experience.

On the streetcar to Art and Vi's, Jeanie told Kenny about their futile attempts at renting an apartment and the possi-

226

CHAPTER TWENTY-TWO

bility they may have to buy a house. "They may want to borrow some money. What do you think? Should we lend them some?"

Kenny didn't answer immediately. *He hasn't changed that way,* Jeanie thought. It always took him a while to answer a serious question.

"I don't know what to say about that. You know more about where we stand financially than I do."

Jeanie was eager to show him the list of war bonds she had bought and their bankbook. She was proud of what she had saved. But last night money hadn't been important.

When they stepped in the door, Merle Ann let out a whoop and sailed into Kenny's arms, but the three little boys hung back and studied him. He hugged Merle and exclaimed, "You remember me!" He grinned at the boys, tousled Buddy's hair, gave Billy a playful punch in the tummy. Then he picked up little Bobby and held him over his head, ducking just in time to miss a thread of drool.

Next he hugged Vi and slapped Art on the back, and all the while Jeanie stood blinking back tears. *Did they feel the full depth of joy that Kenny was back,* she wondered, or were they, like her, not able to get in touch with their feelings. They certainly looked happy.

"You grew." Vi said.

"Yeah," Kenny laughed, "wider, but no higher."

"You get in any tight spots?" Art asked Kenny when they were seated around the kitchen table.

Kenny shrugged. "Naw, nothing like the infantry. But I did have a couple little scrapes. One time, we had an accident with three trucks. I was riding in the back and I flew out and got the wind knocked out of me, but that was all. A couple other guys got hurt pretty bad in that one."

As Long as I Have You

Jeanie interrupted. "You didn't write about that!"

He shrugged. "There were a lot of things I didn't write about. One time we were in tents, and when I woke, there was a spear of shrapnel sticking in the ground about a foot from my head. Another time, when the buzz bombs first started coming over, something went haywire with one and it came down in our camp. I didn't have time to do anything but duck behind a gas tank."

Art roared and slapped Kenny on the back. "Thataway boy. Good, safe place."

"Man did I feel stupid. You can bet I got out of there fast."

"Did it land near you?" Jeanie asked.

"Naw, it landed out on a field and fried a cow." It was good to see a brief flash of his old humor.

"A cow!" Vi exclaimed.

"Yeah, we were right out in the country. Ray told me, when they were in France, they had a cow for awhile and every time you looked around someone was milking her."

"That was really great that you could visit Ray when he was in the hospital in Paris," Vi said.

He nodded. "That was the craziest thing. As big as that hospital was, the first bed I saw—there was Ray. Boy, they treated me swell. I got to sleep in a bed with sheets—in pajamas yet. And they brought me breakfast in bed."

"Couldn't you have faked a terrible headache or something and stayed awhile?" Art asked.

"No thanks. It was fine for a couple nights, but I was sure glad to be able to get out of there and walk around Paris now and then during the day when Ray needed to rest."

Vi poured hot coffee for everyone. "You got to see a lot of Europe, didn't you?"

228

CHAPTER TWENTY-TWO

"Yeah, I sure did. You should see the mountains." He smiled as if he could still see them in his mind's eye. "Sure would like to go back and enjoy them." His smile disappeared. "I'd like to see some of those towns, too—see if they ever built 'em back up. In some places, houses were nothing but a pile of stones and wooden beams, and people were still living in 'em. I can't imagine how they'll ever rebuild some of those cities."

"What about the Battle of the Bulge?" Art asked. "Did you get tangled up in that?"

"That's just about it. Everyone was tangled up. I was behind the enemy lines a couple times, but didn't get into any trouble. We were hauling gas and ammunition up there day and night, right through Christmas."

Jeanie slipped away to the bathroom. She had read some of these things in his letters, but it was different hearing him tell about them. Now she could picture him there.

When she opened the bathroom door, his laugh rang down the hallway. She caught her breath. Suddenly, it was like a connection was made and the feeling she had groped for was there. She leaned against the door frame as waves of joy washed over her. Now her heart, not merely her head, knew—*Kenny was home.*

229

Twenty-three

The joy Jeanie had felt when she heard Kenny's laughter at Vi's was soon tempered by the uncertainties of the future. For one thing, she didn't tell him how much money she had saved. Would he want just to have a good time instead of saving it for important things? She needed to know.

That evening when they got home from Vi and Art's, she took a deep breath, took the bankbook and her record of savings bonds from a drawer and sat down beside him on the sofa. "Want to see what we have?" She held the bankbook open.

He whistled. "You're kidding! Didn't you buy any bonds?"

"Of course." She showed him the list.

His arm tightened around her. "Man! I told the guys you were saving, but I didn't know how much. Where's a pencil?"

She handed him one, and he did some quick figuring on the back of the bond list. "Looks like we've got about thirty-five hundred dollars. You saved my allotment and a lot more."

She felt her face flushed. He was pleased. But now, what would he want to do with the money?

"What are you earning a week now?" he asked.

"I take home about twenty-four dollars."

"We still pay seven dollars a week rent?"

She nodded. "The government froze rents so landlords couldn't raise them."

He laid down the pencil and paper. "I don't know how you feel, but I can't see us just blowing our money. You've worked too hard saving it. I'd just as soon we went on living pretty much like you've have been doing, until we see how things shape up. What do you think?"

Tears sprang to her eyes and she nodded. "I think we should just wait and see." She buried her face in his chest. "I was so afraid you'd want to just go and live it up."

"Since when? Don't we think alike? Remember how many times we'd write about the same thing?"

"Uh-huh," she nodded, but she wasn't at all sure they thought alike. *What about those vulgar words*?

After a few quiet moments she said, "I have to go to work tomorrow morning and tell my boss I won't be in until after Christmas."

"Until after the first of the year," he corrected her. "Let's go up home in a few days. Can't make the folks wait much longer."

She agreed, but she still had some pressing doubts. "Kenny, what if I get pregnant right away?"

His arms tightened a bit around her. "We'd manage."

"But we'll need my wages. If Charles and Thelma decide they need these rooms, we'll have to move, and we don't own any furniture."

CHAPTER TWENTY-THREE

He laid his finger over her lips. "You worry too much. You know God doesn't expect us to have the future all figured out. We're supposed to trust him. Man, I sure had to. Most of the time, I didn't know where I was going to sleep, or where my next meal was coming from, but I always had a safe place to sleep, and I never went hungry very long."

She snuggled against him. "You're right. I'm always trying to plan too far ahead. I guess I don't trust God as much as you do." She sighed. "I want to, though. When you get to know Charles and Thelma, you'll see how different they are. It's like they really know God. I want to know God like they do."

When she left for work the next morning, he was still in bed. She longed to kiss him, but she didn't touch him. He needed to sleep as long as he wanted to.

On the streetcar she saw many of the same people she rode with every morning. Did they have any idea how her life had changed since her last ride with them Friday morning?

She settled down in her seat and stared out at the familiar buildings along North Avenue, as she had done hundreds of times. Their weekend together seemed more like a dream than reality. And now what? All those dreams about taking a trip, buying a car, getting a larger apartment, and eventually a house were no closer to being fulfilled now that he was home. There were no cars available if they wanted to buy one, and with all the servicemen coming home there was little hope of getting a larger apartment for a long while.

Why did I think that we could have and do all these things just because the war was over and he was home? How stupid.

At work, she immediately found Henry. She didn't have to say a word.

233

Henry grinned as soon as he saw her. "Ah-ha! He's home."

She smiled shyly. "I didn't know it showed that much."

He squeezed her shoulder. "I'm glad. When are you coming back to work?"

"The Monday after New Year's."

"Fine." He waved and walked away.

Jeanie found Kate in the washroom.

"He's home." Jeanie said, and Kate threw her arms around her.

"Oh, I'm so glad. Tell me all about it while I change."

Jeanie told her how Kenny had simply walked in Saturday evening. The rest of the story came out in bits and pieces as fellow workers patted her shoulder or squeezed her hand and told her how happy they were to know Kenny was home.

When Kate had changed into her work apron, they walked up the aisle past Jeanie's idle machines to Kate's section.

Kate's eyes probed Jeanie's. "How do you feel?"

Tears sprang into Jeanie's eyes. "I don't know! Oh, I'm happy, but it's like the feelings can't get completely through to where they're supposed to be. The last few weeks I just felt sort of numb and I still feel that way. But one time, over at his sister's house, I came out of the bathroom and heard him laugh and I really felt elated." She toyed with a spool. "But then it was gone again."

"Don't worry. It will take you a little while to get in touch with your feelings."

"And he's so rough. He hurts me every time he touches me. He used to be so gentle."

"Give him time, my dear."

234

CHAPTER TWENTY-THREE

The bell rang, and Kate stood with her hand on the starting button of a machine. "Can you stay a little while?"

"Sure, I'll help you change a rack while we talk."

The noise level grew as machines were started, and they had to raise their voices to hear one another.

"Another thing that really bothers me," Jeanie confided, "is his language. I'm shocked at the vulgar words he uses, and he doesn't seem to even notice me wince when I hear them."

"Oh, I don't think he'll talk that way very long. Pretty soon those words will bounce right back at him."

"I sure hope so. I'm wondering too, when he plans to go back to work. I've heard of so many guys who just want to play around; I guess I'm afraid he won't be in any hurry. He did say he thinks we should just see how things go before we start spending the money I saved."

Kate picked up an empty spool and held it thoughtfully. "I've never met Kenny, but from what you've told me, I think he'll go back to work soon. He doesn't sound like the kind of guy who will sit around and let his wife support him."

Jeanie nodded. "You're right. Oh, Kate, I do love him. I want him to be happy, but I'm afraid he'll think life back home is dull after having seen so many places and having experienced so much excitement." Kate laughed. "Who says your life together will be dull?"

"And I keep wondering if I made good use of my time while he was gone. I wanted so much to make that time count, and I can't see that I've done anything." She looked pleadingly at Kate. "Did I waste all that time?"

Kate straightened up and smiled. "I don't think you will be able to answer that question for a long time. Often, the most important accomplishments don't show."

235

AS LONG AS I HAVE YOU

Back on the streetcar Kate's words came back to her. *The most important accomplishments don't show.*

She wasn't sure what Kate had meant. *Did she mean that I accomplished things that can't be seen—like being able to face other challenges with more courage because I went through these trying years?*

She wanted to talk with Kenny about what Kate had said, but she could just imagine his response. He'd pretend to be serious, but the next minute he'd say something that would let her know he was much more interested in thinking and talking about the present and the future than in probing the past or getting into anything profound.

Nevertheless, she couldn't wait to get home. What freedom. No work for days and days, and they would be together hour after hour.

The door was locked. Jeanie fumbled for her key wondering where Kenny had gone. It wasn't even ten o'clock.

On the table was a note: Gone fishin'. Love, Kenny.

She chuckled and shook her head. She knew he hadn't really gone fishing. He had something to do, but she had no idea what it could be.

The bed was neatly made, and not even a stray sock remained on the floor. His coffee cup was in the sink.

When he still wasn't back at noon, she made a sandwich and ate it while she paced from the front window to the kitchen door. *Where has he gone?*

"I thought I was through waiting," she complained out loud when he still hadn't come home at two.

She settled down and addressed envelopes for Christmas cards and wrote notes telling everyone the good news that Kenny was home.

Chapter Twenty-Three

It was nearly three when he bounded up the stairs. She caught only a glimpse of his grin before he kissed her.

He hung up his familiar camel's hair topcoat, fished something out of its pocket, and led her to the front room. "I had a little shopping to do," he said, "but after that, I went over to Dryden Rubber Company to see if I still had a job."

He pulled her down beside him on the sofa bed. "You're lookin' at a workin' man. I go back right after the first of the year."

Why, she wondered as he kissed her before she was able to reply, *had she been the least bit concerned about his going back to work?*

"Now, close your eyes," he told her with an excited glint in his own.

She heard paper rustling before he took her hand. When he slipped a ring on her finger, she could no longer keep her eyes closed. Sparkling next to her wedding band was a diamond solitaire. "Oh, Kenny, it's beautiful."

"It's pretty small; you like it?"

She threw her arms around him. "I love it, but I don't understand. I thought we weren't going to spend our money on things we don't really need."

"We aren't. I didn't spend any of the money you saved. This was money I saved." He took out his wallet, and showed her two dollars. "I spent everything but these. I wish it could have been bigger, but I didn't want to wait, 'cause I figured you'd talk me out of it if you knew. You didn't get a diamond when we were engaged, so I wanted you to have one now."

"I never dreamed . . . I couldn't imagine where you were." Her kisses thanked him.

That night, snuggled against his shoulder, she told him about that dark night, so long ago, when she wasn't able to see the way back to the house and how, through these trying years without him, life often seemed that dark. She told him how light gradually came as she looked out beyond herself and determined to make good use of the time they were apart. "Kate says the most important accomplishments don't show. Do you think that's true?"

He raised up on his elbow and stared at her in mock seriousness. "Oh, she is so right," he said and kissed her passionately.

Deep inside, as his kisses became more urgent, Jeanie chuckled. *He is the same Kenny.*

She awoke before he did the next morning, leaned on her elbow and gazed at his relaxed face. She was about to smooth his heavy eyebrows and kiss him, when he opened his eyes and stared at her. "I thought I was dreaming," he whispered and drew her to him.

She smiled against his shoulder. Already he was becoming more gentle. Feeling the pulse in his neck against her forehead, all her concerns about the future lost their urgency. For now it was sheer bliss to simply absorb the reality of his presence.

She knew life's dark nights would come, but no longer would she have to grope her way through them alone.

Kenny was here.

And God never felt closer.

To order additional copies of

As Long
As I
Have You

send $10.99 plus $3.95 shipping and handling to

Books, Etc.
PO Box 1406
Mukilteo, WA 98275

or have your credit card ready and call

(800) 917-BOOK